LOVERS
IN THE
FOG

A Novel

Hamlet Sarkissian

PAGE PUBLISHING, INC.
New York, NY

First originally published by Page Publishing, Inc. 2019

ISBN 978-1-64424-150-9 (Paperback)
ISBN 978-1-64544-601-9 (Hardcover)
ISBN 978-1-64424-151-6 (Digital)

Printed in the United States of America

For Nathela

"Toil on, son, and do not lose heart or hope. Let nothing you dismay. You are not utterly forsaken. I, too, am here--here in the darkness waiting, here attentive, here approving of your labor and your dream."

Thomas Wolfe, "You Can't Go Home Again"

LADIES AND GENTLEMEN, if there are any ghosts, angels, spirits or any other mysterious creatures riding along with me in this car, listen carefully. I have something very important to tell you.

I met a woman ten years ago. We had the most passionate love affair that you could imagine. Then she disappeared. Just like that. Vanished from my life with no trace, no explanations. Why, I've always wondered. I hadn't heard from her in ten years, except for two missives she sent me, photos of herself from the days when we were together. There were no messages attached, just the photos. Why didn't she want me to see her the way she looked now? Why send me photos from the past. What had happened to her? I didn't have a clue.

Then a week ago, out of the blue, I got a letter from her. Just a one-sentence note. She wanted to meet me in the same place, a little bed and breakfast in Montauk called Martha's Inn, where we had tasted happiness together for the first time at the tip of Long Island.

That was ten years ago. Ten years ago was in the last century. Dear and honorable ghosts, angels and spirits, what do you make of that? Suddenly out of nowhere, she re-appears. Does that make any sense to you? Of course not! Say it! This sounds like a bad dream. Or tell me I'm a lunatic who has always lived in my own head. See me driving day and night up the eastern coast of the entire United States of America to meet her again? All because of a one-line note after ten years of silence! You must all be thinking that I should be confined to an asylum. Right? Be honest with me. I get it. I've heard it before.

I've got news for you: I still love her.

Did I say that? Oh, God, I swear, I'm tempted to make a U-turn and go back home. Maybe I will. It's so hot in this goddamned car. It's raining or I'd open all the windows. I'm speaking loudly but I can't stand my own voice.

I remembered a railroad crossing near Miami, on my way to the I-95. The blinking red lights announced an approaching train. Suddenly the window wipers bounced into action, back and forth, cleaning frantically. I turned back and stared at my vacant back seat.

Hocus-pocus. Hallelujah. Which one of you did that? Man, you're one determined silent crowd, aren't you? But thanks anyway.

My wipers could hardly keep up with the assault of hard rain that was falling. Out of nowhere, penetrating through the rain and fog, a locomotive emerged, lumbering down the tracks pulling scores of freight cars. I watched them pass and disappear. Still contemplating the idea of a U-turn, I hesitated to move forward into the misty tunnel of fog shaped by the car's headlights. Idling the engine in the middle of the road, I kept staring at the blinking red lights at the crossing long after they had turned green.

Maybe I should turn around. I was afraid, okay? Yes, I'm afraid. Say it again. I'm afraid to meet her again. I am. I'm not hiding it. She must be afraid too. But I had to admit she was one hell of a gutsy woman to initiate this adventure.

Why did she want to see me again? I was so glad she did, but why? I'd waited for her and fantasized about her for so long. What was I saying? I didn't even know what the hell I was feeling about her at this point. I just knew that not knowing was hell on earth. So I kept driving northward toward our rendezvous.

I made sure the car's fog lights were on. My lights barely penetrated the white fog. All I could see was whiteness in front and whiteness behind the vehicle. I've never liked the color white. It has always scared me. For many years, I wondered why angels, God and the rest of the creatures from Heaven Inc. always appeared in white. For some reason, no other colors were in fashion up there.

Why couldn't God sometimes dress up in red or blue or orange, for Chrissakes? Neither did I ever understand why all the saints, angels and the rest of the flock so blindly followed His sense of fashion. My confusion persisted until I realized that the dead also come in white. Everyone from the underworld showed up in white too. So eternal life and death came in white? Those two mortal enemies, the opposing forces of nature, were the same? What a contradiction! It was confusing, to say the least. What a lack of imagination! So where did God come from? From below or from above? From above, I was told repeatedly and never questioned it. That was until I started living that same contradiction in my daily life.

"God, are you up there now?"

"Yep."

"How's the weather?"

"Raining."

"God, do you know what love is?"

"I'm the one who created it."

"Are you dressed in white now?"

"Yep."

"God, are you upset with me? Just be honest."

Silence.

"God?"

Suddenly You're silent again. God, I asked if You are upset now. Of course You are. Because You know what's going on in my heart, right? You don't approve of it. You think I should be with my wife and my child now. Instead, I'm on this godforsaken road, driving through the fog, confessing my love for a woman I met ten years ago but couldn't forget.

THIS MORNING HAD been difficult. Despite the magical Floridian sunlight and the soothing sounds of ocean waves not far from our house in Key West, things were tense.

"Luke?"

Margaret's voice was jittery, full of worry and doubt. Her trademark firmness had been steadily eroding for some time now. I was staring into space, lost in thought.

"Are you feeling okay, honey?"

"Yes, what time is it now?"

"You have time. Aren't you going to eat anything?"

"No. I should get going."

"Should I make a sandwich for you?"

"I'll get something on the road."

Julian, my 7-year-old son, displayed his empty plate to both of us.

"I'm finished."

"Good boy."

"Daddy, if we put two pieces of bread on the sun, they'll get toasted, right?"

"Yep," I said. "You can even call your new dish organic cosmic toast."

"Hey, Mommy, I want organic cosmic toast tomorrow."

"Give us a minute, honey. Mommy and Daddy have to talk now."

I gathered my things and put on the blue coat that went with my blue suit pants. I had decided to make the journey by car, explaining that I needed some solitary time to sort things out in my head.

Ostensibly, I was going to New York to interview for an attorney position opening at Akin, Bailey and Johnson.

"I looked them up," said Margaret. "It's a prestigious law firm."

"I haven't got the job yet."

"You will, Daddy," offered Julian.

"Of course you will," said Margaret. "You're going to be a human rights lawyer again. Call me after the interview and let me know how it went."

I didn't respond. All three of us started walking towards my car.

"Don't forget," she added, "we need to go to that book launch party for Nicholas on Saturday."

"He'll do fine without me. It's his show."

"You've been through so much together. We should be there to support him."

"He'll do fine without me, honey. But I'll try to be back in time."

Margaret stared helplessly into my empty hands.

"Where's your bag?"

"He forgot it again," said Julian, smiling. "I'll get it for you, Daddy."

"Come here."

I hugged Julian hard.

"Daddy, don't forget my choir concert next week, too.

"I won't."

"Love you, Daddy."

"Love you too, my son."

In the driveway, Margaret hugged me for a long time, despite the rain. I don't think she believed I was really driving all the way to New York for a job interview. Anything that came out of my mouth was suspect. I'm not sure if she knew where I was really going, but if she did, Margaret did a damn good job of hiding it.

Julian ran out of the house and handed me my bag that I'd left in the living room.

"Thanks, Julian. Now both of you get out of the rain."

Momentarily, I could see Margaret's lips and hands trembling. Julian of course didn't notice her fear. As always, she kept her torment to herself and pretended to smile.

"Take care of yourself, my love."

She didn't want me to leave.

Oh, God, what was I doing? I don't even deserve her. What I was doing was not fair to Margaret. But I had no choice. None whatsoever. I had to do this.

Abruptly, I got into my car and drove away.

Margaret was waving good-bye with tears rolling down her cheeks. Julian held his mother's hand. I looked at the two of them in my rearview mirror and could only imagine that exchange between my son and my wife:

"Mommy, why are you crying?" asked Julian. "Daddy's coming back soon."

"It's because I already miss him."

God, You said You created love. Did You create this special love for me? Don't You feel some responsibility here? Are You watching over me? Or are You only watching over people who wore white? I'm wearing blue today, so no one is watching over me, right?

Look, do me at least one small favor.

Give me a break with the goddamned rain, will You?

3

THIS BRUISED PANASONIC voice recorder has been with me for the last ten years, registering my disorderly stream of consciousness. She gave it to me. Because of her, I'm in the habit of recording myself all the time. Some might find it peculiar. Going back to the days when I was working for human rights groups, it's something I had to do all the time. Every lawyer uses a voice recorder now and then. Though I'm no longer working in human rights, I haven't been able to kick the habit. I record what I'm thinking and then listen back to my own rambling thoughts. It's as if there were two of us: my thoughts and me. It seems I needed to hear my own words again just to understand what they meant when I thought them up.

Isn't it strange that the self inside talks to you in a whisper, so insecure and frail? So full of doubts. Quite the opposite of the loud, pompous, outside self who's talking into this little machine, the guy who sounded so confident, educated and therefore supposedly knowledgeable.

Knowledgeable, my ass.

That guy knew shit. I mean nothing. Zilch! Let's get real. That guy spoke volubly, yes. But being voluble didn't necessarily mean he knew what the hell he was talking about. He acted as if he did though. That's the way of life I suppose. I confess I hated his voice. I mean I hated my own voice.

She didn't. She was somehow in love with my voice. She had me sing lullabies to her. She wanted my voice to be her memory of night. At the time, I thought it was silly. Now I see those lullabies were precious. I tried singing them to other women. Every single one of them laughed at me and made fun of me for doing it.

Forty times I have been around the sun on this old Earth. No matter where I had launched any of those 40 orbits from, I always ended up a year later in the same exact spot. We always begin and end in the same place. It's as simple as that. Some of those years were more amusing than others. Some of them I didn't even remember. I might've been sleepwalking, hung over or just plain emotionally numb. Maybe the sun wasn't hot enough. I couldn't feel its life-giving warmth. No wonder I felt so exhausted and somewhat baffled about my cosmic experience.

Only during the last ten of those year-long circles had I begun asking myself questions about the meaning of my own existence. Every time I discovered an answer, it confused me even more. It was a lonely exercise.

After each Q&A session within myself, the almighty awful loneliness crawled deeper inside my body, metastasizing in a more brutal and cynical fashion. Until one day, I realized that there's no such thing as loneliness. Or solitude. You're never alone. You carry the world within you at all times, the world that you've created for yourself. I wasn't lonely anymore. I was never lonely. I was just blind for a very long time. A whole world was riding along within me at this very moment.

I discovered that the true secret of the "not-being-alone syndrome" was to confess to yourself. Become your own priest and your own sinner. It was the most important thing for you to do. When you become your own god and your own demon, or rather your own judge and your own prisoner, you'll never be alone again.

MY FELLOW GHOSTS, angels and invisible spectators, I know my car is hot and you all want nothing more than a breath of fresh air. So do I. But it's raining hard and so the only Atlantic breeze is coming up through the car's vent system, turning the brisk air warm. Anyone want drinks? Candy? Jolly Ranchers, Hershey bars? C'mon, pick your poison! No? Are you sure? Okay then, buckle up and allow me to introduce myself.

My name is Luke. Luke Forsythe.

This morning, I began my trip appropriately on Route Number One, known as the Overseas Highway, cruising northward in the fog and rain through the Florida Keys up toward Miami. It's a 113-mile stretch of mythical roadway with water stretching out on both sides. I had the strange feeling that I'd been driving there all my life, endlessly gliding above the ocean on those impressive concrete piers. First built in 1912, the Overseas Highway was a historical landmark. Today I made my own personal history there. At least that had been the plan. Except as I drove this morning, I was lost. When I say, I was lost, I don't mean geographically. I mean emotionally lost.

I never knew how to handle my emotions. They've ruled over my life for as long as I've been conscious of myself. And just when I thought I was supposedly mature enough to free myself from their tyranny, I was about to fall into another, even bigger black hole. And I thought I was finally getting stronger!

The reality was that I didn't know anything about handling emotions or black holes. All I knew was that I was traveling up this foggy road to see her again.

I had missed her so very, very much.

The fog swallowed up all the traffic signs. Millions of gallons of mad raindrops were cascading down from the darkened sky without a break. Cars and trucks traveled cautiously. From late fall to early spring, fog can blanket this part of the world unexpectedly. Neon lights from a big ship off the coast glittered momentarily in the misty distance, and then fell away as my black Volvo station wagon rolled on.

When I passed Islamorada, I glanced into my own rear mirror and caught sight of a very tired man. Yes, I'd only started the drive that morning, but the night before, in anticipation of getting started, I couldn't sleep a wink. I flipped the mirror up so I couldn't see myself.

When I looked at my face these days, I was shocked to see the person looking back at me. I'd changed so much that I didn't even recognize myself anymore. I wondered why it was such a distressful sight.

Was it because I had another image of myself in my head? A younger, more joyful version of me? The me I used to be? Or was it because I was getting older and in denial. Both were fairly immature, self-centered thoughts. Thoughts like those that we usually ascribe to women of a certain age.

At least I didn't have to share those kinds of thoughts with the rest of the world. If people could hear each other's private thoughts, like on this voice recorder, we'd have unending wars between the sexes. But maybe we wouldn't be such hypocrites. And maybe we'd come to terms with our own deceitful natures and find some peace within ourselves. An eternal, deep, primordial peace that humankind had never ever experienced.

Whatever the real reason was, I no longer could look into mirrors. Mirrors seemed to be in conspiracy with time itself. They reminded us that life had passed us by, that it was fleeting, that everything was temporary, that time could not be stopped.

5

AFTER KEY LARGO, the rain mellowed on the mainland. I had been on I-95 a little while, but needed gas and a break. Out of the fog, the glowing silhouette of a gas station appeared like a phantom. I pulled in. The station's bright fluorescent lights radiated off the fog. Their whiteness was blinding. I had to wipe off the moisture on the gas pump window so I could read the current price of $1.40 a gallon for diesel. Inside the attendant's booth, a middle-aged man in a work uniform was on the phone, apparently having an argument with the person on the other end. Suddenly he yelled something and slammed the phone down, smashing it into bits and pieces of broken plastic that flew all over the booth. I turned my eyes away and filled up my tank, then walked to the booth to pay. I knocked gently on the window.

"Do you know how long this fog is going to last?"

"How would I know?"

"You probably live around here, I thought you would."

"It just sticks around. Sometimes for weeks."

"See, you do know."

The attendant gestured as if he was in a hurry. Yet the place was as dead as the surface of the moon.

"We're not far from the ocean, so obviously we're going to get fog. You're not from around here, are you?"

"Did I say something wrong?"

"My wife just asked me for a divorce. How would that make you feel?

"Angry. Disappointed."

"Exactly. Are you going to pay for the gas or not?"

"Sure. I'm sorry about your wife."

I handed the attendant some cash.

"We've been married for 27 years and now she wants to leave. She says she's fallen in love with someone else. We've got three grown-up children, for God's sake!"

"Matters of the heart are mysterious."

"Mysterious, my ass! It's pure selfishness. She used me while she needed me. Now she doesn't need me anymore. She's found a younger lover. My family was all I had. What am I going to do now? This is shit. It's so fucked up that I want to toss a match at this fucking place and blow it up. I was in the army, you know."

Seeing him getting more and more agitated, I tried to change the subject.

"Do you still sell engine oil here?"

"All kinds."

"Castrol 20-50, please."

I opened the hood while the attendant went inside the station and re-appeared with a new can of oil in his hand. He looked me straight into my eyes.

"Are you married?"

"For ten years now."

"Do you love your wife?"

"Yes, I do."

"Me too. I still love my wife. That's what's so fucked up about it. But I'm such a shit. Never really appreciated her. And now that she wants to leave me, suddenly I do appreciate her. Suddenly I'm afraid. I don't want to become one of those bitter old men who die in loneliness. I can't live without her. But it's too late. Hey, I've just told you the truth. If I tell the truth to a total stranger, why can't I tell the truth to my own wife? Maybe I'm afraid of love. Does that make me a coward? Why was I afraid to show her my love? Why?"

I stared at the attendant with a vacant look, lost in my own thoughts.

"But do you know what hurt me the most? When she told me that she'd found new happiness with this young man, a happiness that she had never felt with me. When I heard that, it was like a knife went through my heart. It's still painful, even now. Hey, have a great day."

The attendant turned and went back into his booth as if nothing unusual had happened. I stood still for a moment in reflection. The attendant opened his window and shouted out to me.

"You'll have fog all the way, but it will get better after Fort Pierce."

Then he shut the window again and started to clean up the pieces of the telephone he had smashed.

The fog was staying with me. I probably needed it.

6

LET'S FACE IT, we were all in a fog. A few days of sunshine here and there, but the rest of our lives we spend in a fog. How can someone's newly discovered happiness become a source of such pain to someone else? How can two people live together for 27 years and feel that they have not yet said everything to one another? That man's pain was so real. It reminded me of my own. But me? I was different. Really? I couldn't even express my feelings. I was a master at hiding my pain. I had hidden it for ten years now. It was so old that I could drink it like fine wine.

The few photographs that she had sent me were from our old days. It was funny calling them "old days." That was such a lie. Those days have never grown old for me. They were as fresh and as vivid and as haunting as ever. Maybe it was the same for her. Or maybe not. I didn't even know if I liked those photographs anymore. I had looked at them hundreds of times, over and over again. Their edges were frayed from my fingertips. They no longer made any sense to me.

With her, I never knew what I liked or what I didn't like. I never had time to think about liking anything. Time stopped mattering. No past. No future. Not even a present. We lived together for moments, or even milliseconds. There were those tiny bits of frozen time when suddenly everything started making sense, when life got under your skin, when you loved so much that you felt both the pain and the divinity of it. It was perfection. A true gift from God.

I loved her too much. But not enough.

Or maybe because it was never enough.

I missed her. I missed all the words that I didn't hear for all these years. I missed all the looks. I missed all the touches and stroking that I didn't get all these years. I missed the trembling of my heart, the dryness of my throat and my shortage of breath. I missed the sparkle in her eyes, her swollen, wet lips, her silky skin covering me in warmth.

God, why was I so afraid of this journey. Why did she want to see me so suddenly? Every time I looked at those photographs, it seemed to me that she had succeeded in freezing time, in my mind at least. They were engulfing me into her time vacuum. What an odd choice for our rendezvous. Meeting again at Martha's Inn?

With her, everything had to be different and unique. No one could figure us out. We couldn't figure ourselves out. Anything that seemed odd to other people seemed natural and just great to us.

For example, we always went back to the same places where we'd made love before. To stare into each other's eyes. Making love again, this time with our eyes. In those moments, I could feel my heart in my throat and my blood pumping in my neck. In those moments, I tasted the sweetness of life on my tongue. But all that honey came afterwards. The first time we ran into each other, it was nothing more than her lonely, gorgeous nymph eyes burning my neck.

Hey, you still want to hear about this? You imbeciles, calling yourself angels, ghosts or spirits! Kingdom of Heaven University attendees? Okay, you're silent again. I hope I didn't put you to sleep with my relentless love sermon. Give me a sign that you're with me, that you're listening to me.

Suddenly I sneezed.

For Chrissakes, I said give me a sign, not your germs!

7

WHERE WAS I? Ladies and gentlemen, I have to admit that I'm a preposterous hypocrite on many occasions, especially when it comes to my memory zone. Just when I pretended that I had to supposedly refresh my memory, the deep, unconditional, cast-iron truth was that I had not forgotten even one molecule of my encounter with her.

As a matter of fact, I tried hard for years to forget her, to erase her from my memory, to wash her tentacles off my skin. But I failed miserably. It was a grandiose failure. Look at me now. Ten years later, driving through the fog on this godforsaken road in Southern Glades, confessing my love to an emptiness filled only with a no-good bunch of journalistic ghosts from the Holy Ghost News Services. How pathetic was that?

The night that I met her was preceded by one of those uneventful days when the dominant driving forces were the dullness of life and the numbness of emotions. The kind of day when you have to drop off the dry cleaning, watch the stock market plunge to hell, shout at the mobile phone billing operator, and try to escape the onslaught of TV news, radios and newspapers, all of them in unison vomiting up silly celebrity news or shiny pieces of spectacular political garbage, creating an unbearable cacophony.

Society and the government were diligently working together to achieve what they thought they were supposed to do: stupefy us, dumb down our kids, reduce life to a spreadsheet and eventually enslave us. My way of resisting the international bankers, military industrial complex, the one world government and all the ruling Socialist elitists was to go after work to a decrepit bar in Brooklyn that had no name. The regulars called it "The Hole," but that name wasn't written anywhere in the establishment. There weren't any fancy cocktail napkins. There was no signage or address. Its whereabouts were passed along in the medieval oral tradition. It was like some men called their wife "My Old Lady," but wouldn't dare write it down in black and white. The Hole was irresistible because it was so austere. Its godforsaken atmosphere accurately reflected my state of mind in those days.

That particular day when I first laid eyes on her was pretty much forgettable. I had been wasting the oxygen supply of Planet Earth by simply breathing. I could just as well have spent the entire day on a respiratory ventilator, like one of those intensive care patients who's brain-dead.

As I was parking my car in the litter-strewn lot behind The Hole, I thought to myself, "I guess this was another stupendously unnecessary day in my life." I wasn't sad or feeling anything remotely like gloom. I'm not supposed to feel or understand anything anyway, no? Given the way our society functions, who can? If you think you do, then you're a fool. Little did I know that my entire life was going to change that very day. I had no idea! Not one goddamned clue!

THAT EVENING, LIKE most of the time in my life, my intuition, or my instinct, or my whatever that Nostradamus device is called was completely turned off. Just thinking about what happened next gives me goose bumps all over. Her eyes are still burning my neck, even now, ten years later.

I walked into The Hole and took my preferred seat at the bar with my back to all the tables and booths so I wouldn't have to see anyone. I ordered a "Holy Grail," their special martini that went straight to the brain. It arrived soon thereafter and I lifted the conical glass, ready to take the first welcome sip, exhaling my last "in the moment" breath of air, as my shrink friend called it.

See, numbing myself with alcohol had proved very beneficial for me. Up to then, the technique had worked, preventing me from killing myself or, for that matter, killing someone else. As Herman Hesse wrote, it gave me a chance to "maybe bother myself with living." Just so you know, the Holy Grail was a local mix that had an international array of ingredients delivering every kind of bitter taste that Mother Nature had created. One sip of a Holy Grail was equal to a fifteen-year stretch in a Chinese communist prison camp. I have seen people taste the Holy Grail, walk out of the bar and divorce their wives. Divorcing their wives seemed easier than finishing up that horrible cocktail. To me, sipping a Holy Grail was an act of piety, theologically overpowering. One swallow was precision bombing into the depths of my soul, killing every single molecule of any emotion. I was like a vacant lot by the end of the night. You could park anything you wanted inside me. I wouldn't feel a thing.

I took the first sip. In the beginning, it went down as usual and it did what it was supposed to do, which was mainly provoking a lot of regrets.

You should know that I'm a highly-trained specialist in regret. It's my hobby. Apart from looking after my sick mother once in a while, I regretted almost everything all the time, including that very moment on my drive thinking back to that night at The Hole.

The Holy Grail worked in a very Catholic way, I thought. The mix of sin and guilt first warmed up my tongue, then went down my throat like a meteor crashing on the moon, making me cough up the healthy spit of my last hopes.

But there was something else this time, other than the olives and cherries I chewed on. My neck started to feel warmer. Suddenly it was burning hot. At first, I thought it was a naughty trick that a guileful martini like the Holy Grail could play on you. But as the moments passed by, my neck started to burn even more. I tried massaging it away with my hand. I even asked the bartender for a wet towel to relieve the burning. Nothing helped. On the contrary, I started to sweat profusely. My neck was on fire!

Then I turned around, looked over my shoulder and into the crowd of patrons. I didn't see her at first. It was smoky in The Hole, full of sex-starved people moving their bodies, some scantily-clad, to Psychedelic Furs' "Love my Way." Through the people on the dance floor, I caught sight of her eyes staring at me. Penetrating through me. I stopped breathing for a moment. Mesmerized by her intensity, I dared to hold on to her gaze. Hers were no ordinary eyes. They were two fireballs burning me up, exploding everything inside. I felt as if I had been struck by lightning. I couldn't swallow. There was no more saliva in my mouth, just a shriveled-up, useless tongue. The metronome inside my heart was hitting *allegro* and *crescendo* at the same time.

I've been shaken up pretty bad in my life. I've seen a lot of incredible stuff. But never before had I felt so excited and scared at the exact same moment. I blinked to make sure my eyes were functioning. What came into view was the most beautiful creature I had ever laid eyes upon. She was so divinely gorgeous, with such a beautiful aura, that I was ready to forgive everyone everything. The pain in my liver went away. So did my stomach cramps. The bottom of my back no longer ached from sitting behind a desk for hours on end in a law office. That first glimpse of her made the arthritis in my joints evaporate like the dew on a rose.

I was spellbound. She jolted me deep down, right to my core. I tried to smile back at her. But my face was out of my control, molding itself into a caricature of myself. My eyes froze. Her stare was fierce and cold as ice. She didn't blink, not once. She was looking through my ridiculous external shell, gazing inside me. Her face was unafraid, impolite, intense. And completely unapologetic.

9

I DIDN'T BELIEVE it. She was actually looking at me?

"You mean you're interested in me?" I strung words into a thought. "But you're a Venus-like goddess straight out of a Botticelli painting."

That gorgeous nymph with mind-numbing beauty and candor was really looking at me? With eyes you could die for? It couldn't be true. There was no way she was the least bit interested in me? I was too petrified with shock and wonder to comprehend what was going on. I smiled and turned away, thinking she must have looked my way by mistake. Then slowly I turned back around and glanced toward her again, as if by accident.

There she was, staring at me the same way! Now her gaze was even more intense than before. She wasn't just studying me, she was inviting me to join her. That look was like a confession and a strip show wrapped into one. It was shockingly bare of pretense. What was I to do? Come on, a beauty like her couldn't be on her own in a place like The Hole?

But she was. She was sitting at a table by herself. No one joined her as she sipped her own fizzy drink, maybe a prosecco, and continued to look straight into my eyes. Her eyes said things more sincere and guileless than any words anyone had ever uttered into my ear.

I couldn't claim to be any Casanova. There wouldn't be any 10,000-page accounts of my triumphs with women. But I had had my fair share of conquests. One might even call it an excessive catalogue of women who I'd encountered in the "Lost and Found" section of life. That's probably because I myself was a long-term wanderer in that department. The usual suspects were always freshly divorced, widowed, abused in childhood, depressed, confused, or recovering addicts. Or they had simply lost their way in life. In short, they all had one thing in common: they were all disturbed women who needed a man who would listen to them and sometimes caress their hair.

When I say "me," I don't mean "me" in an egotistical way. I mean I was simply all the above in one person: divorced from reality, widowed from my work, struggling with my own addictions, abused by the system, confused about everything.

Usually we'd end up having sex a short while later after getting to know each other a bit more. We would have a very warm, passionate yet sad departing night. And then we would move on with our lives, having become a couple twice-divorced, twice-widowed, twice-confused ad nauseam. Who wanted that situation? No one did.

I liked this arrangement. Wet lips. Dry lips. Big tits, small tits. Big squishy asses, small tight asses. You name it, I had tried them all. I was a sort of social worker/lover, medicine man/ass grabber.

Soon I got tired of my unholy ladies' man role and switched to imbibing alcohol instead. It was so much more fun. Being a Westerner, a human rights lawyer and going on assignments in Eastern Europe didn't help. How do you cope with so many beauties having such hard lives in such deeply broken-down societies? You either kill yourself or you drink and have sex. Because there's nothing else you can do. You can't change a damn thing. If you think you can, you're a fool anyway.

By then, I'd firmly intellectualized my heart, covered it with plaster and placed it on display inside the museum of my body, right above my liver. It was there, working away, pumping blood. But I never felt its beating. To be honest, me and my heart had formed a very cozy, peaceful coexistence. It would take care of functioning at its own regular rhythm and I wouldn't bother it with unnecessary emotional upheavals.

But that was in the past. Now exactly at that moment inside The Hole, as this goddess was turning my insides out and upside down, my heart was throbbing like a Holly Roller on crack. My heart was pissed off. Angry as hell. And terrified too. I had never betrayed it like this before. I'd always honored my end of the contract. I'd always taken good care of it, protecting it by walking away from relationships that might become complicated. I turned off the TV when orphans from some godforsaken hellhole of a country were emaciated and asking for food. And my precious heart always rewarded me with the peace of mind that my tired body was yearning for. Me and my heart had this wonderful, mutually-respectful, beneficial bond of brotherly love.

The catch was that my calculated, society-educated and society-nurtured relationship with my own heart had turned me into a selfish bastard. Everything was getting mixed up inside me and I was slowly evolving into a Model Citizen. That's the last thing you want to become. Because if you do, it meant that you had accepted this immoral, idiotic, greed-based, sex-obsessed, materialistic society, a structure that we were all forced to participate in. "Model Citizen" meant that your enslavement process had been successfully completed, that you'd transitioned into a product/consumer. Then they would chip away at you and dispose of your being at the appropriate time.

Well, not me, not yet, goddamnit. As long as I was in The Hole drinking volatile martinis named after a biblical artifact, I was still free. I was a true outlaw, a revolutionary. I was my own man. At least in my own mind.

Plus, that particular day was different. Finally, I had good news for myself. Today, for some mysterious reason, my Nostradamus' device was switched on. The Holy Grail was working perfectly. As I drank one and then a second, they were telling me that my heart wasn't supposed to feel comfortable, it was supposed to feel emotion, for Chrissakes.

"Don't be afraid, my son," I heard it saying clearly, "Jesus, the Holy Spirit and the Virgin Mary are all with you. What else do you want? Not one but three gods are there. Break away. Break away from your comfortable contract with your heart. It's fake and disingenuous."

I stared back at her, directly into the depths of her eyes. It was like someone had tied a 10-ton stone to my neck, handcuffed my wrists, duck-taped my mouth and pushed me into the deepest part of the ocean. I was drowning, ladies and gentlemen, drowning in her world. I wanted to cry out "adieu" to my peaceful days. But my heart, now vengeful, was piercing my chest from the inside.

What the hell was going on here? Who was I? What did I mean by asking, "Who was I?" I had never asked that question of myself. Just by staring at me, this woman made me question my very being. How could a look do that to me?

God, are You still around?

My Nostradamus' device was about to switch off again. With one last desperate effort, my heart begged me to turn it off and archive it back in the museum of my soul again. It was too late. No more resisting her. Give in, goddamnit. Live your goddamned life. Go and love that woman. My knees were already moving and my feet were tracking toward her. It was too late for any more misgivings.

First, I circled her table. Then carefully and cautiously, I took a seat next to her. I said hello, attempting to greet her confidently. But for some reason, no audible sound came out of my mouth, only hot air. I heard my voice from inside, but she didn't answer me or even look at me. She simply looked past me into the smoke-filled bar. Abruptly, she stood up, picked up her purse and walked away from the table.

I was in shock. I tried saying, "What the hell?" but my lips still made no sound. I was flabbergasted. I was furious. This woman was over the top. This goddamned pathetic woman had been staring at me non-stop for maybe half-an-hour, teasing me, inviting me, seducing me. She'd made me break my contract with my own heart. She'd made me question my entire existence. And now she'd ditched me in a heartbeat?

"Thank God you walked away, woman!" I said loudly to no one in particular. But I liked the sound of my voice. That was me. I was back. I let out a sigh of relief. She had disappeared into the crowd. I went back to the chair at the bar on shaky knees.

"Another Holy Grail, please," I said to the bartender.

I really liked my voice sounding confident again. "I almost lost you," I thought to myself. I was about to start apologizing to my heart when suddenly I spotted her standing in the far corner of the club, right next to the back door. She was staring at me again. But now her stunning lips were shaped into a Mona Lisa smile. There she was, seemingly waiting for me, offering me all the treasures of her beauty with her eyes.

To say that I was confused is to undermine every single letter in that very important word. I was so bewildered it felt like I'd lost my mind. I looked around the room desperately seeking an ordinary face in the crowd, someone with whom I could strike up a superficial conversation, full of inconsequential, mindless crap. My eyes searched in vain and then I glanced back at her. Sheepishly I looked into her eyes one last time before she opened the door, stepped outside and took my free will with her. I threw some cash on the bar counter and followed her out.

THAT NIGHT, BROOKLYN'S waterfront was unusually quiet, its streets empty. A light rain was falling and fog was creeping in from the harbor. The eerie silence was interrupted by two sets of footsteps, hers and mine, echoing one another. She walked along in high heels. I wore the alligator cowboy boots that I got on the black market in Yugoslavia which were now part of my standard bacchanalian uniform back in the days when I frequented The Hole.

The dense fog diffused the lunar light but the mystical full moon still owned the night. The world had turned pale white except for her yellow dress and purple high heels. I couldn't take my eyes off of her figure until the fog swallowed her up.

I had x-rayed her silhouette, trying to imagine the hidden treasures beneath her clothes, while my nose caught a whiff of her luscious perfume. Never before had I been so aware of man's kinship to our four-legged Canis Lupus brothers hunting in the wild. Suddenly I was a lone wolf with a hyper-sensitive nose, smelling the world through her, tracking her scent. Listening intensely to her every footstep, my ears tingled and pricked up. They were suddenly covered with fine fur.

Then I started howling. I heard the howls from inside. But just like back in The Hole, my mouth formed the shape it needed to cry out a mournful shriek, yet nothing audible actually came out. All I could hear was the clicking of her high heels and the sound of her dress rubbing up against her bare legs. The rest of the world didn't really matter. Not even me turning into a wolf mattered.

Useless questions flashed through my mind. Who was this woman? What was she turning me into? Was I going to come out of this night alive? Answers were meaningless. In that moment, the truth no longer meant anything. That moment was the only truth that mattered.

She turned onto Love Lane. You've got to be kidding, the street name was right out of a B movie. She paused and listened every so often to make sure that I was still on her trail. The fog broke and that's when I caught sight of her and the childlike smile spreading across her face. It was as if she couldn't believe her good luck, like a little girl who was about to get her favorite toy. The tiny, two-star hotel that she walked into had a blue-and-red-colored neon sign above its door that said, "Stardust Hotel." The sign was old and worn out like the place itself.

By the time I reached that decrepit establishment and went into the lobby, she had vanished. There was no one at the front desk. I heard the soft click of a door handle somewhere down the hotel's long, narrow corridor.

Cautiously, I walked to the end of the corridor. Maybe this was a set-up for unsuspecting idiots who get sucked in by seduction gambits just like this and end up relieved of their money and credit cards. The door to the last room on the corridor had been purposefully left ajar. Foolishly, I pushed it open all the way and went inside.

WHAT HAPPENED NEXT was one of those moments in life that you keep coming back to over and over again. Every time you visit the movie theater of your memory, a new detail or sensation from that experience dawns on you. Every single time the scene screens, you wonder how you could've missed this or that important detail. I saw that particular film in my head for many years to come.

I had always loved going to the movies. Especially the ones inside my head. My movie theater wasn't grandiose, certainly not a multiplex or anything like that. It was tiny and run-down, like the Spectacle Theatre on South 3rd Street in Williamsburg, its seats stained from years of buttered popcorn, soda and fruit juice. Just like the Spectacle, I always chose the same seat on the left side, in the back row of my brain. The films I watched were varied, coming as snippets since they were mostly memories. Sometimes they screened as vignettes, sometimes in incoherent bits and pieces without a narrative. There were also prolonged frozen moments without movement, nothing more than an emotion hanging in the air. I adored them all. I was willingly trapped inside that movie theater. I'd volunteered to be taken hostage without anyone to negotiate my release. It was great to not have a future, to become a prisoner of the present. What happened next in that room at the Stardust Hotel would become vital footage in my own personal cinematheque.

Except for a few slits of milky moonlight slicing through the Venetian blinds, it was totally dark in there. Outside, I could make out the silhouette of the Brooklyn Bridge looming high above. I heard her breathing but I couldn't see her yet. My eyes hadn't yet adjusted to the darkness. I moved toward the bed in the center of the room and sat down cautiously. The bedspread had a velvety texture. When I leaned back on my hands, I realized that my palms were sweaty. Since childhood, that has been a red flag for me, a sign of self-preservation. Sweaty palms meant that warning lights were blinking simultaneously all over my body. Circuits were about to be shorted out and an explosion was imminent. It was my body's primal signal that my insides were stirring with excitement and that trouble lay ahead. It was me telling me that I should stand up and immediately walk out of the Stardust Hotel. But I didn't.

I heard her moving onto the bed behind me. I froze. All my doubts vanished in a heartbeat. I had no time to get away. Time had stopped. She came up from behind and covered my eyes with her hands. Her palms were moist, too. Compassion for her swept over me right away. I wanted to say, "I know how you feel, my love."

"My love"? Yes, my mouth was ready to call her "my love" right then and there. But not me. I was too scared of those words. You see, my mouth is a survivor. It had said many things, good and bad, violent and sweet. My mouth had gotten away with plenty and it had been punched around as well. It had bit and spit and licked and suckled and chewed. You name it, my mouth had done it. Even though I didn't know how to deal with life, my mouth did. I'd always envied my mouth for knowing how to handle both pain and pleasure. My mouth was a risk-taker. But not me. All I could manage to whisper was, "What's your name?"

Her hands were soft and tender. They smelled of lavender. Her fingers glided down over my eyes and cheeks until they rested on my lips.

I obeyed without a question. The ensuing silence was exciting and terrifying. From somewhere she brought out a black silk scarf and the next thing I knew, she was tying it over my eyes, securing it with a tight knot in the back of my head. Then she started slowly unbuttoning my shirt. When her lips softly touched my chest, they were so soft that I didn't feel them at first. But as she began to cover my body with more passionate kisses, my chest warmed up and welcomed her.

I raised my arms and tried to hug her. She immediately stepped back out of my reach and placed my hands back on my knees. I understood that I didn't have permission to touch her. Not yet. Her lips went from my chest onto my shoulders, then they circled around my neck and finally ended up on top of my head. I have never been kissed so thoroughly, so meticulously. Yet I had no permission to kiss her back, nor touch her.

Her lips caressed my upper crown chakra, the one that every book claims to be about spiritual well-being, the purple chakra on top of the head represented by a thousand petal lotus. The experts will tell you that that chakra was our connection to the gods. But those know-everything gurus, those keepers of the secrets of the Himalayan mountains, never mentioned the goddesses. When this goddess kissed my upper chakra, I didn't become a spiritual being, I turned into a wolf again, a wild animal. I felt like running on four legs, wagging my tail and showing my teeth. Suddenly I had the intense desire to start howling.

Feeling so primitive was both relieving and empowering. Life seemed so much simpler. My one-track mind wanted to take her completely. To lick her face. To dominate her. There was dirt under my fingernails. I smelled blood. Suddenly my neck started twisting one way and the other. I got chills all over my body. And an inexplicable smile stretched across my face from one ear to the other. I was feeling powerful, my muscles were swelling and blood was rushing down my neck like a wild river.

SHE WAS NOW undressed. I felt her nude body radiating heat and desire after being freed from her dress and underwear. She pulled the scarf off of my eyes. It took me a few moments to see her in the faint moonlight oozing through the blinds. There she was at the top of the bed reclining against the pillows and headboard. Naked. Her body was screaming beauty, perfect in all shapes and colors. Her skin shone in the dark, beaming an inner light. Just looking at her made me fall apart. Bits and pieces of me were toppling into a black hole. I took a deep breath and tried to balance myself before my chaotic descent into nothingness. It was useless to resist her.

She smelled of love. With every breath, I inhaled her, taking in as much love as my lungs could hold. She had poured red wine into two coffee cups and now gave me one of them. I saw in her eyes that she didn't want me to touch her yet. She just wanted me to look at her and take her in with my eyes.

In my time, I had seen a great many mortal women naked. In various places, with various lighting, and sometimes under creepy circumstances. Few had served me lousier wine than this cheap $4.99 merlot she had poured for us. Yet I had never seen a naked goddess before. My eyes scrutinized her breasts, her thighs, her knees, then went back to her mouth, her nose, her eyes, then down her bare legs to her tiny feet. It was so strange that all of her seemed so familiar to me, as if I'd been born into the delightful landscape of her body. I had a feeling that I'd spent my youth in between her thighs, my childhood between her breasts and now, as an adult, I was returning home to take over her lips.

Suddenly she started giggling. The sound of her laughter was so crystal clear, it was almost biblical. People sounded different in biblical times. As they had no noise back then, no cars, no airplanes, no traffic, they heard one another differently. I was hearing her in that way, so clearly it hurt my ears. Her laughter was loud and contagious. I couldn't contain myself. The situation was as funny to her as it was scary to me. She laughed out of joy. I started laughing out of fear. But we laughed together. Naked. On the bed, laughing, desiring one another, still laughing.

Neither of us had any words to utter. You know what I'm talking about? Those important sounding combinations of consonants and vowels that we all use to communicate with one another? They had vanished, just gone. They had disappeared without a trace. We didn't need them. Words were smart enough to see what was happening and voluntarily left us alone. We didn't have to speak. Our bodies were talking for us. Our eyes, our hands, our souls did the talking. She took my hand and placed it on her breast. Her lovely round nipple was tender. I was feeling the life source underneath. I cupped her other breast. Her breasts felt precious and electrifying. She reached out softly for my shoulders and her eyes locked onto my eyes. She seemed to be searching for something. Something very deep and mysterious, something unknown to me. Like lasers, her eyes surgically removed all my protective layers, one after another, until she found what she was looking for. Whatever it was, I could see the discovery had put her completely at ease.

She smiled slyly. Then she kissed my hand. This goddess had crowned me as her master and now was making me feel as if she were my slave. Her thighs opened slightly. She gently dipped a finger into her wine and placed it on my mouth like a gesture of forgiveness. I licked my lips. My tongue confirmed my nose. It was that pitiful $4.99 merlot that's made from the "widow grape." You find it in supermarkets in the cheap wine section. It was usually on sale and known for provoking bitter tears.

The vintners who made that wine should have been thrown into jail for stopping the fermentation process prematurely with sulfates in order to hurry their product to market. Instead of soft and velvety, this Chateau Screw Top stuff was harsh and aggressive. It was a sacrilege, not only the vintage, but for what I was about to do with the goddess after we set the coffee cups down on the nightstand.

She had taken a drink of that dreadful wine but didn't swallow it yet. I thought that was because the stuff was so bad she couldn't drink it. But after swishing the merlot around in her mouth, she spewed it out and erupted into kinky laughter. The crimson liquid splayed all over her breasts and belly. Suddenly tears were rolling down her cheeks, then her wonderful face flashed a broad grin. She was laughing and crying at the same time.

She moved closer to me. I stopped thinking about the lousy merlot when her tongue hungrily slipped in between my lips. She pushed deep inside my mouth, up to my brain. She was dripping wet. We were swept away into the open sea. There was no help to be seen for a million miles around. I thought I might as well drown quickly. And I did.

13

I OPENED MY eyes early the next morning. It didn't feel like the next day but more like a millennium or two had passed by me. I felt light as a feather, ethereal. A strong wind could've blown me away.

Most importantly, she was no longer next to me.

Light ropes had been attached to my wrists. Her black silk scarf was still around my neck. I had lipstick all over my body. Later I would discover in the mirror some bite marks and bruises on my neck. I had no recollection of being tied up the night before. That type of crap had never appealed to me anyway.

I tried to recapture the events of the night before moment by moment. The problem was that my mind seemed to go blank right after our first long kiss. The hangover didn't help. Clearly there was a road block in my upper chakra. I jumped out of bed and looked in the bathroom for her. She was long gone.

As I hurriedly got dressed, I noticed $300 cash conveniently placed on top of the nightstand. Wait a minute, that wasn't my money. What was that about? Could it be? What? I couldn't believe that I was thinking that she'd left the money as some sort of payment? She'd paid me for sex?

I sat back down on the bed, stunned. I thought we'd had something thoroughly special together. But she'd left me money as if I was a whore. She'd treated me like a fucking prostitute. I couldn't even begin to comprehend that. I was so humiliated. She must have set it all up. Yeah, she'd picked me up at The Hole, arranged the cheap wine and the scarf and led me to the shittiest shit-hole in Brooklyn, the Stardust Hotel, to have her way with me. Everything had been

40

planned out. Why would she do it? I had to find out. I couldn't let someone treat me like a whore and get away with it. Thank God I wasn't a woman. Is this what they go through? I had never understood it before then.

My blood pressure went up like an intercontinental missile. Clearly I couldn't leave that hotel room intact. Look, I'm prone to violent outbursts. Inside I'm an angry man struggling to tame the beast. Nowadays I'm much better at subduing the wolf that lives inside me. But at that goddamned moment, I couldn't stand in its way.

Neither could I damage that shitty hotel and cause the kind Indian family who owned it any more headaches than they already had. I decided to do something stupid but symbolic to show how I felt. I found a thin metal spoon inside a coffee cup that was stained red from that horrible merlot. Clearly she had planned it all around that fucking coffee cup. I took the spoon and twisted it violently, then doubled it and doubled it again. Finally I bent its head back and forth until the metal gave way and it cracked off. Then I tossed the headless wreck of a spoon back inside the cup and walked out.

I COULDN'T BELIEVE how quickly I would forgive her. After all, she was a goddess. Who would ever have dared to pull off such a stunt? I was hooked. I was intrigued. I was also terrified. I knew I'd fallen in love with a stranger. I didn't even know her name, or who she was, or for that matter, if I'd ever see her again.

She'd taken a piece of my heart and I didn't know what was she going to do with it. Nothing was more terrifying than to have someone abandon your heart in some unknowable place out there. Maybe it would just be dumped on the side of a road. Or plopped down on a pedestal in a museum in full display for everyone to see. Thinking about the possibilities made me want to scream. Maybe I should scream now. But what good would it do? It might even blow out my recorder's microphone.

After Jacksonville and well into Georgia, there was a detour sign on I-95, so I took US-17, a smaller road that cut through the Georgia countryside parallel to the highway, still blanketed with some light fog.

When I felt myself getting drowsy, I pulled over and stopped under a road sign that had appeared out of the fog. I walked around my car for some fresh air and paused underneath the wordy road sign above my head. I took out the little flashlight I always carried in my pocket and shone it up at the big sign so I could see it clearly.

"We're glad Georgia's on your mind," it said. "Savannah, 50 miles. Smiling faces, Beautiful places, Charleston, 140 miles." Atop the sign was a CCTV camera, its lens sparkling when I pointed the flashlight up there. A separate smaller panel announced, "Entering Ricoboro, the City of Pride."

I lit a cigarette and stared at the surveillance camera pointing down at me, shaking my head in bewilderment. I decided to do something about that damn camera. I opened the trunk of my car and grabbed a hammer from the toolbox. Then I climbed up on the railing next to the road sign, reaching as high as I could, and swung the hammer at the surveillance camera. I shattered the lens. A second swing struck the device's plastic base and smashed it into pieces. The CCTV camera drooped, its lifeless body hanging down, swinging from its video cable.

I climbed down on the ground and looked at my handiwork. It started to rain again. I turned on my voice recorder.

"Good people of Ricoboro, City of Pride, thank you for your welcome. And to all those between here and Savannah, and all the citizens of Savannah, which was just an hour drive from here in this godforsaken weather, I am touched by your hospitality. But it's nobody's goddamned business if I am driving through your neck of the woods, or what I am doing with my own life in my own country. Do you all hear me? Good. I take your silence as a sign of agreement."

Refreshed, I got back into my car and started the engine. I let it idle for a minute and reflected. I should turn back, no? I was acting like a madman, so maybe I should go home now and salvage my life. But I had already come this far.

I got back on the empty road, my headlights slicing through the rain and foggy darkness on either side. Maybe the power had been cut in northeast Georgia. As I approached Savannah, the street lamps on the road weren't working. Everything was dark. Only black in front and black behind me. A pitch-black vacuum.

I hate the dark. Never liked the color black since I was a kid. Throughout one's lifetime at every important occasion, they force you to wear it. We graduate in black, marry in black, die in black. Priests are dressed in black, politicians are in black, the devil is in black. Vampires are in black. Prostitutes, stock market brokers, bankers, judges, shamans, magicians, professors, cops, even waiters, for Heaven's sake, are all dressed in black.

Basically, man's world is in black and God's world is in white. Black and white. Any color in between makes you feel like a pariah. Black is scary. It's colorless. I suppose you have to be scary to be respected. Dress in red, green or yellow and you might as well join the circus. Everyone thinks you're a clown. Or an eccentric tourist. Or that you have simply lost your mind and your manhood.

All you Saturn and Satan worshippers, you black magic practitioners! You treat the world as if everyone is supposed to belong to your secret society or at least obey the rules and regulations imposed by your mindfucking rituals.

Not me! I am my own man. My own rebel. I'll have my own revolution every day. I'm going to break your fucking rules right now, at this very moment. Who says I have to be in a fancy suit and tie and $600 black Weston shoes and a fucking Patek Philippe watch with a white gold band? Fuck all your status symbols! I'm out!

While I was driving, I took off my jacket, then my tie, then my shoes and my tailor-made shirt, always keeping one hand on the wheel. The car swerved a little across the middle of the road, but no cars were coming the other way. With my left hand on the wheel I tossed my shirt, jacket and shoes onto the back seat. Now I was topless and barefoot behind the wheel.

"Freeeeeeedom!" I screamed, driving my car on that lonely road with the wind blowing on my naked chest. I felt I was a step closer to my real ancestors. If only I could hunt at night. That's when the great hunters went hunting, the most fearsome ones. They said if you could hunt at night, it meant the spirits of the ancestors were with you. You were in line to become a chief.

I pushed down on the gas pedal with my bare foot. The car's speedometer started climbing. The wind and rain rushed by, moaning like a wounded animal. I found myself screaming even more with savage excitement. Then suddenly in the rear-view mirror, I glimpsed a police car coming up behind me with a loud siren and lights flashing madly.

I slowed down and pulled over. The police car braked to a stop right behind me, flashing lights going round and round methodically. The officer got out and approached the passenger side of my car carefully, his hand on his gun holster. He was overweight, with a thick moustache covering his entire upper lip. I rolled down my window.

"I'm sorry, officer," I said.

"Driving license, registration," said the policeman.

"Officer, I apologize. Really I do."

"Do you know how fast you were you driving, sir?"

"I'm not sure."

"100 miles per hour! That's nuts in this weather!"

"It certainly didn't feel that fast."

"Oh really, it didn't feel that fast, huh?"

The policeman shoved a breathalyzer device in front of my face. "Blow into this. Now!"

"I haven't been drinking."

"We'll see about that. Just blow."

I did as I was told, but the breathalyzer needle rose no further than zero.

"I told you so," I said, relieved.

"Why are you half-naked?" said the officer. "Behind the wheel?"

"Got tired of my clothes and shoes."

"Are you on any medications?"

"No."

"Do you have any drugs, herbs or any other mind-altering substances in this vehicle?" asked the officer as if reading a script.

"No."

"Do you mind if I take a quick look?"

"You're not supposed to. Not without a search warrant."

"What? You some kind of lawyer?"

"Yes, matter of fact I am," I said. "But I don't mind at all, just for this one time. Let's get it over with."

The officer circled the car, opened and closed the trunk, came back around and shone his flashlight into the back seat.

"Hey, officer. Be careful with that flashlight in the back seat."

"Why?"

"I have invisible passengers riding with me in this car. There's a ghost, an angel and a spirit. All three of them are back there, sleeping."

"Invisible passengers, huh? Think this is some kind of joke? This is going to cost you."

The officer handed me my Georgia speeding ticket.

"You'll remember me when you pay this!"

"Freedom is priceless, officer."

15

THAT NIGHT WHILE I was rolling up the East Coast, a book-signing event was happening in a Key West bookstore called New Horizons to mark the publication of "Unsung Heroes: Dispatches from Behind the Iron Curtain" written by my pal and human rights specialist, Nicholas Cooper. The book was published by Prometheus Editions, which was started by Jim Moore, a wealthy New Yorker – a free-thinker and political radical – who had also launched New Horizons as a haven for booklovers. Jim had done everything he could to generate as much buzz as possible in the community for the new book. A good crowd of about 100 people showed up for the event.

Margaret arrived late that night for the launch party, so she came in through the back entrance from the rear parking lot. Nicholas had already begun his presentation, standing behind a small lectern in front of the screen filled with a bright slide of the book cover for "Unsung Heroes" featuring a photo of the dissident Vasily Verbitsky. There was a woman on the cello in the far corner providing soft background music, playing Aram Ilyich Khachaturian's *Andantino* with a soft, elegant touch.

Margaret sat down in the back of the bookshop as quietly as a mouse. Nicholas glanced at her appreciatively and continued his presentation.

"…Back then," he was saying, "Luke Forsythe and I were proud to call ourselves human rights lawyers. But I don't think I understood that human rights are more than just ideals until the Vasily Verbitsky case.

"Human rights are everyday people's desires to free their minds from tyranny and secure liberties for their spouses and children, Jefferson's 'self-evident truths,' that we take for granted here in the West. In autocratic and undemocratic regimes, the desire to live free can lead to torture and death.

"The reason I wanted to write this book with several years' perspective was to document the incredible struggles that we witnessed. Teachers, students, mathematicians, engineers, workers — ordinary people — calling themselves dissidents, took extraordinary actions, jeopardizing their lives and the safety of their families in order to be able to speak the truth, regardless of the authorities.

"Many of them were battling within the framework of the USSR's constitution. Not Vasily Verbitsky. He was a scientist by trade who became a self-taught constitutional expert whose underground treatise about constitutional law landed him in jail and…"

Nicholas turned and pointed to the screen over his shoulder. "…on the cover of my book."

Abruptly, the cellist stopped playing and put down her bow. She was sobbing. Everyone looked over toward her.

"That's okay, Marina," said Nicholas. "I'm so sorry. This must be hard for you. Ladies and gentlemen, Marina was married to Vasily for 10 years. We are fortunate that she was able to emigrate to our country and be with us today."

"Please excuse me, Nick," said Marina, putting down her cello and covering her hands over her eyes.

"I hope all your eyes will be opened by the book," said Nicholas. "I'm pleased to sign your copies and answer any questions. Thank you all for coming."

There was warm applause, people got up and started moving toward the author's table that had been set up for Nicholas to dedicate books. He waved at Margaret from the lectern and then weaved through the crowd to where she was standing. They exchanged a warm hug.

"I kept expecting Luke to heckle me. Where is he?"

Before Margaret could answer, Jim Moore approached them.

"Any sign of Luke Forsythe yet, Nicholas? I've got journalists who want to talk to him, so he'd better not pull one of his vanishing acts."

"Margaret, this is Jim Moore, my publisher. Jim, Margaret is Luke's wife.

"Hello."

"Mrs. Forsythe, a pleasure."

"Luke's at home in bed with the flu," said Margaret, lying masterfully. "It's unfortunate, I know, and I'm very sorry. Maybe he can do some press over the phone. You know, when he's better?"

"That's too bad," said Jim, disappointed. "I'll let the journalists know." Turning to Nicholas, "What about the Russians? You promised me at least one real live dissident.

"Jim, you promised me a review in *The New York Times* and *Washington Post,*" said Nicholas. He then walked over to the author's table, sat down and started signing copies of his book that people had purchased. He turned and whispered to Jim Moore: "There are Russians here, but you need to stock up on more vodka if you want real dissidents."

Margaret turned and observed Marina mournfully placing her cello inside its case. Their eyes locked with long-awaited curiosity, exploring each other for a few beats. The two women were eager to talk to one another, but suddenly the weight of the situation in the bookshop seemed heavier than either anticipated. Still, Marina broke out of her conundrum and approached Margaret.

"Excuse me, are you Luke's wife?

"Yes."

"I'm Marina. Marina Hagopian. Vasya was my husband."

"Yes, Marina, I'm happy to meet you at last."

"Luke's here too?"

"No. And honestly, he doesn't talk about anything from those days. I really want to know more."

Marina seemed lost in her thoughts for a moment. She picked up a copy of "Unsung Heroes," turning to the photo section in the center of the book. She held up the page to show Margaret.

"Here's Luke with Vasily, Lev, Tolya and me."

Margaret stared at the black and white picture for a long moment, then said:

"I've heard Vasily's name before."

"Did Luke talk about Lev or me?"

"Not really."

"I thought tonight we could be together, all of us, happy for Nicholas. He has done so much for us. I mean he and Luke got us to America. I'm so grateful to both of them." Marina closed the book and looked at Margaret solemnly. "There's so much to talk about, I don't even know where to start from."

Tears started rolling down Marina's cheeks.

"I… I mean we all miss Luke…but…"

"But what, Marina?"

"He's been avoiding us recently."

Margaret was surprised and intrigued.

"Do you know why?"

"No, I mean maybe because me and Lev are now…" Marina was unable to finish her sentence.

Nicholas came back around to the two women after signing books, an inebriated little smile on his face.

"Hey, I'm glad you two finally met. Margaret, can you drive me back? I think I'm drunk. I couldn't resist the wine or the vodka. Actually, I drank both."

MARGARET DROVE ALONG the night-time streets of Key West slowly. Nicholas rode shotgun, enjoying the cool ocean breeze. They turned into Whitehead Street. Margaret pointed at a Spanish colonial house.

"That was Hemingway's place."

"I always wanted to see it. Didn't Tennessee Williams live here too?"

"Yes, he did, much longer than Hemingway. But Papa had the bigger house. Williams lived in a cottage on Duncan."

"It's like D.C.," explained Nicholas. "It doesn't matter what you do as long as you have a big house. You throw one big fund-raising party, they'll remember you and ask for contributions until doomsday."

"It was a good launch party for your book, no?"

"I hope so, but I'm glad it's over. Now we can actually talk. Why don't you tell me where the hell Luke really is? Have the two of you had a fight?"

"He's gone."

"Gone where?"

"I don't know. He came up with a pretext for leaving, but who knows the truth."

"What?"

"He's been distant. He barely speaks to me. I knew something was up. He took off yesterday morning, supposedly for some job interview, but hasn't called me and he didn't say when he'll be back. He's not answering my messages. What am I supposed to think?"

"Margaret, having you in his life is what keeps him going. You give him hope."

"Apparently not anymore."

"You know how much he loves you. He'd never hurt you."

"He's already hurting me."

Margaret pulled the car over onto the shoulder of the road.

"Do you think he went to see her?"

"What?"

"I mean how can I compete with her?" Margaret broke down into tears. "I don't know what to do. I can't take it anymore."

Nicholas put his arm around Margaret and hugged her. He held her for a few moments, gently kissing her hair. Delicately Margaret moved away from him and looked directly into his eyes. She said:

"There's something I've always wanted to tell you. I knew, I mean, I've felt this before. That you wished we were together." Margaret took his hand. "Right? Please don't deny it. I feel it's time for everyone to be honest. What I need now is clarity."

Nicholas turned a little pale, but remained silent.

"I wanted to tell you once and for all. You're a dear friend. But if I went off with you, I would end up thinking of Luke all the time."

"Sorry, Margaret, I'm…"

"I'm sorry, too. Please help me with Luke. I'm worried."

"Now I know why he's been avoiding me."

"Thanks, Nicholas, which hotel are you in?"

"Ocean Reef Club, please. 764 Barracuda Lane. I'll get some sleep and then fly myself back at the crack of dawn."

"With a hangover?"

"Don't worry about me. I just got a new Cessna. It's a lovely little plane. I'm going to come back and take you and your family for a ride."

"Help me with Luke," said Margaret, sighing. "Please. I can't go on like this."

"I promise I will."

The car stopped in front of the Ocean Reef Club. Nicholas kissed her on the cheek and hopped out. Margaret drove away.

MY CAR WAS parked on the side of the road next to a place called Folly Beach. The water was calm, shimmering with a silver quilt of light. Still bare-chested, I was walking across the sand.

This was Charleston, South Carolina. That meant I was 741 miles away from my home in Key West. I'd driven about 15 hours, including rest stops, and had another 874 miles to go to reach Martha's Inn in Montauk, New York. So I was almost half way there. Folly Beach, said the road sign, was the "Edge of America." It was a perfect place to take stock for someone like me who was half-way through life, a guy who'd been on the edge of collapse for almost a decade now.

When your life is on the edge, you think a lot about matters of life and death. As our old friend Billy Shakespeare so eloquently described it, "To be or not to be." I guess Shakespeare needed to simplify the dilemma for the working class folks who came to his theater so they could absorb his message. He didn't want to frighten or confuse them with grandiose statements. Good old Billy was a great entertainer. His audiences came first. He didn't want to hurt their trivial feelings or make people feel too uncomfortable. Billy was a gentle guy. He let his audience believe that they had a choice, that they could choose "to be" or "not to be", even though he knew very well that for anyone to attempt the "to be" option truthfully, they had to seriously contemplate the "not to be" option first. But then, why complicate life so much? It was just a play, just some actor pre-tending on a stage whether the character he was playing was willing to go on with his miserable existence or if he wanted to take his own life and end it all at once.

For God's sake, that had nothing to do with your real lives, my dear audience, and that includes you Elizabethan ghosts, angels and spirits with your embroidered costumes and puffed-up hair-dos on the back seat. You do not have to ask such unworthy questions in your real lives. All right, let's have the mad prince ask the big question on the stage. Did Shakespeare seriously think that you had to be mad to ask such essential questions? Why couldn't Horatio ask it? Was it because Horatio is the voice of reason? Did Billy mean that you had to be an unreasonable human being to ponder the worthiness of life? If I was asking that question now, does it mean I was on the verge of madness? Well, according to the most celebrated writer of all time, I was. Who was I to argue with Shakespeare?

I wasn't really sure. All I knew was that everything here, right at this moment, on this sand, was so real and so vivid that I had the overwhelming sensation that time was a floating thing. Time moved like the sea waves in front of me. You could ride on time forever.

Yet time was making me feel a little seasick. It was infinite and irrelevant. Time didn't age or change. Time was like a freezer. It kept emotions fresh.

Then how come right now, right this very moment, I was re-living my life from 10 years ago. Moreover, I was re-living it in two parallel realities, both here and elsewhere at the same time. To be geographically exact, I was simultaneously at the "Edge of America" and in Soviet Russia before the demise of the USSR.

By the way, if you are one of those who's focused only on those daily exchanges between society and your own ego, where you track your material wealth and power position like a stock market chart, stop reading this right now.

Continue only if you have a daily brain fog in which you are continuously living and re-living, questioning and re-questioning your past, present and future, all at the same time. Welcome to my world.

I WAS SENT to Leningrad by Hartman, Cooper and Stein's main power partner, Nicholas Cooper. As Gorbachev's perestroika[1] and glasnost[2] were shredding the inhumane fabric of the communist dictatorship, Nicholas had the brilliant idea of illuminating a younger generation of dissidents in the Soviet Union by teaching them about law.

Nicholas wanted us to teach them about all kinds of law, be it constitutional, criminal, civil or property, raising and grappling with issues about liberty, privacy, social equality, democratic participation and human dignity. As the undemocratic Russian empire along with its secret prison system was coming apart, Nicholas Cooper's project was to bolster the construction of a better society.

It would finally be possible for the Soviet people to have a better country without the gloomy shadow of cannibalistic Bolshevik ideology, where Russians didn't have to eat each other up just to survive. At long last, they could put an end to the prisons of Lyubianka and Matrosskaya Tishina where the best and the brightest, generation after generation, had been locked up in dungeons whose keys were thrown away. Inside those prisons, you were either tortured or given the infamous "9 kopek" verdict, which made reference to the cost of the single bullet that was fired into the back of your head.

---

[1] The meaning of perestroika is "restructuring", referring to the restructuring of the Soviet political and economic system.
[2] Literally "publicity," it was made popular in the 1980s by <u>Mikhail Gorbachev</u> as a slogan for increased government transparency.

All that was about to end, thank God. Finally, liberty for all and a law-abiding society. Our hope was that producing enough food and goods for everyone would also produce peace and prosperity. Something that people living in the sprawling Russian steppes had never experienced.

According to Nicholas, there would no longer be any need to wage hot or cold wars, and we could all live in peace and harmony in a law-abiding society.

Did I believe that? Yes, maybe I did. I certainly wanted to believe it.

When Nicholas asked me to get involved with him and told me about the opportunity in Leningrad, I saw only one way to respond: "Let's get to work!"

Our job was to organize conferences about identifying voters, doing opposition research and winning elections. We would be teaching young Russians how a real government works, a government elected by the people where there are checks and balances to power, a government guided by ethics that are clearly identified and regulated by laws restricting each branch of government. How about free markets and election technology? Talks on all that were in the works, too.

Most importantly, the International Institute of Human Rights asked me to write a report on the abuse of political prisoners in Russia, an assignment I immediately accepted with Nicholas' blessing. Basically, I was supposed to get the names of any remaining political prisoners and smuggle the list out and into the hands of respected journalists in the West so that those fearless individuals would be recognized in important publications like *Le Monde* in France and *The Washington Post* in the United States.

The reasoning behind this project was simple and powerful. At some point, every criminal is looking for a measure of respect. By the late 80s, Soviet politicians were being treated in the West like the assholes and bastards they were. Suddenly, they became aware of their own images. For the first time, they were conscious of the West's assessment of their conduct. If we could identify political dissidents, those bastards in the Kremlin would leave them alone. At least, that was our theory.

My job was to get media attention for people in the dissident movement, be they doctors, physicists, teachers, writers or civil servants. It was a matter of life and death to get their names out there. The Soviets had persistently claimed there were no political prisoners in Russia. It was the government line ever since Khrushchev famously announced in 1959:

"We lock up only criminals and the mentally ill, not political prisoners."

Everyone knew the leaders were lying in order to cover up their sinister activities. As quickly as possible, I had to find out who the dissidents were and get them recognized internationally. Nicholas introduced me to my first two dissidents, Vasya Verbitsky and Lev Horowitz. Both men were highly regarded specialists in their respected fields: Vasya was a thermonuclear physicist and Lev was the senior art historian at the Hermitage Museum. Both of them immediately promised to help identify others. What brave people those first two were to even consider cooperating with me.

As I talk about that time, it all feels like a movie. Suddenly I'm back in my own cinema seeing my life as a film again. Except this time, the film's in color with an enchanting voice in the background singing a Russian folk song, a tune that I was not able to get out of my head for a decade.

LEV HOROWITZ'S GAZ-21 Volga was a pretty comfortable sedan. I realized right away that it was an exact copy of a mid 50s model Ford Mainline. However that long-ago night, neither of my two fellow passengers knew about the remarkable similarity between the two vehicles. That was because the only American cars Lev and Vasya had ever seen were those brief shots of vehicles in Russian propaganda movies where poor black people were always being exploited by fat, white slave-holders.

The Bolshevik propaganda machine had really never moved past the Civil War era in U.S. history. Of course that was intentional because anything prior to the Civil War had to include the Declaration of Independence, the Constitution and the Bill of Rights. Those documents were gigantic leaps forward not only for Americans but for all mankind as well.

In addition, anything after the Civil War had to portray the greatest economical progress in all the history of recorded civilizations, thanks to liberty, trustworthy government and lawful taxation.

For 70 years, Soviet people had been fed the lie that their collectivist regime was the only hope for the oppressed peoples of the planet. God forbid expressing any other worldview. If you dared do that, you were the opposition, the 5th Column, a counter-revolutionary, and a fascist, even though fascists were socialists too. But worst of all, you would be labeled "Enemy of People."

That moniker sounded more like a B-movie from the West about monsters and goblins than a serious category for government opponents. Nevertheless, at that time within the Soviet Union,

"Enemy of People" was the most frightening tag any citizen could be given. And there, driving with me in this Soviet Volga-Ford copycat car were two former political prisoners who wore that label proudly. They considered themselves patriots and the Communist state as the real "Enemy of People."

While he was driving, Lev opened his third beer and started singing along with a melancholic song on the radio entitled Tyomnaya Noch[3], which fit the occasion perfectly. In the back seat, Vasya and I were tossing back shots of vodka, but I could hardly keep up with him. Evidently Vasya had serious expertise in this activity, making me feel like a sophomore wanna-be drinker, the same guy who was nicknamed "Dean Martin" by my fraternity brothers at Yale in admiration of my excessive consumption of any and all alcoholic beverages.

But Vasya! In one hand, he held not one, not two, not three, but four vodka tumblers in between his fingers. He filled up each one of them with vodka, stopping the pour exactly three centimeters below the rim. Despite Lev's stop-and-start driving and the road's potholes, Vasya was able to knock back all four glasses without wasting a drop. It was a performance worthy of one of those death-defying acrobats at Cirque Du Soleil.

"Sip vodka, don't shoot it," he said. "Smell the vodka as you swirl it in your glass. Exhale through your nose to fully appreciate its aroma. And then you can swallow it."

I told him, "Hey Vasya, your eyes are turning as read as the Soviet flag."

"It's on purpose, Luke," he replied, "so that me and my country finally can understand each other."

"I have a joke," injected Lev from the front seat.

"Go ahead, illuminate us."

"Lenin is making love to Kroupskaya, his wife. Lenin says, 'Comrade Kroupskaya, did I hurt you?' She says, 'No Vladimir Ilyich, why do you ask?' Lenin says, 'Because you moved.'"

We all started choking on our laughter.

---

[3] *Dark Nights.*

"You moved?" repeated Vasya, splattering my face with crumbs from a sandwich he had been eating and spraying me with vodka. But then his laughter turned into a prolonged cough attack.

"Let's drink to the wives who know how to move," said Vasya, opening another beer. "My wife, Marina, should read more about Kroupskaya."

Vasya started laughing so hard I thought he was about to have a heart attack.

"Hey guys," I said, "what about my seminar? I was supposed to organize one here, teaching about governance, free market economy and how to win elections."

"Whoever gave you this assignment must've been drinking terrible *samagon*.[4] Sometimes when that stuff is not brewed at the right temperature, it can be toxic."

"Are we going to talk about anything else but vodka?"

"Cognac?"

"I'm serious. The seminar could be very helpful. You people are about to reform your entire society."

"You're not another Dean Reed, are you?"

"Who is Dean Reed?"

"You don't know who Dean Reed is?"

"No."

"We called him the 'Red Elvis.'"

"Never heard of him."

"He was an American rock star from Colorado who came to the USSR believing in Marxism-Leninism. When he got disillusioned and suddenly wanted to go back home, his body was discovered floating in a lake in East Germany. Of course, Stassi had nothing to do with it, right Lev?

"Right.

"You're not a Marxist-Leninist, are you, Luke?"

"Not one bit. I'm a Jeffersonian Republican."

"That's why we are drinking with you. Otherwise we'd end up at the bottom of that lake alongside you."

---

[4]   Russian for moonshine vodka.

Suddenly I turned pale and erupted into an uncontrollable bout of coughing myself.

"Are you okay?"

Seeing me unable to breathe, Lev pulled the car over.

I scrambled out of the car onto the side of the road where I started vomiting my guts out. I was shaking terribly too. Vasya held me around the waist so I didn't fall on my face, which he was splashing with cold water.

"No more vodka for you, my friend, no more vodka. Oh, God, we thought you could drink!"

"You call that shit vodka?" I managed to say in between more convulsive vomiting.

Lev handed me a paper towel to dry my face and dabbed another towel around my mouth. Suddenly I could breathe again.

"I'm all right now."

"Do you want some beer?" asked Lev.

"I didn't vomit enough?" I shouted feebly. "You people are crazy. I don't know what I'm doing here."

20

FINALLY WE ARRIVED at Anatoly's birthday party.

It was happening in a cafeteria called Stolovaya on Mokhovaya Street, right next to LGITMIK.[5] I was there with a group of typical Russian intelligentsia, engineers, teachers, doctors, writers and journalists. Everyone was drinking more vodka. Except me.

Vasya was so drunk he couldn't stop laughing and Lev was about to make a toast. Lev would always come out with one of those toasts that are told like fables. You heard the story, and then at the end you drank to the moral of it. Drinking in Russia was the most moral thing you could do. Being moralistic was allowed and encouraged as long as you had a glass of vodka in your hand. To give his toast, Lev got up on the table with a teacup full of vodka in his hand. He raised his voice to get everyone's attention.

"Comrades. Friends. This one is very serious. Listen up! Imagine three trains on parallel tracks speeding towards the same final destination. The three trains are called the Past Train, the Present Train and the Future Train. Most people always choose one of the trains and ride it until the end of their lives. That's where you see people who live only in their past. They keep complaining about what happened to them all throughout their lives. They never see the present and never think of a future. These people are scared of progress and they continually refer to 'the good old days.' Do we have a Past Train passenger among us?"

---

5   Leningrad Institute of Theatre, Music and Cinematography.

Everyone looked at Anatoly Govoroukhin, a mathematics professor at the State University who was sitting at the end of the table.

"What?" said Anatoly, nervously lighting a cigarette. "I don't live in the past. Why are you all suddenly staring at me?"

Everyone burst into laughter.

"C'mon Tolya," said Lev. "Look at the way you're dressed. People wore suits like that after the Second World War. That was decades ago."

"So what if it was decades ago?" said Anatoly. "People had style in those days."

"Yes, but look at your shoes, your haircut. Everything is from those days. It's like you refuse to live in today's world."

"What's there to like about the today's world? Rampant corruption in our society? Degradation of all our moral values? Lies and manipulation by the authorities?"

"Shush, Tolya. Have you gone mad? Be quiet my friend. If they hear you, you're finished and all of us are going down with you. There's no point in getting agitated. We're having a good time here. Maybe you're right. But who cares? Nothing can be changed anyway. Still, you look like someone who's coming out of the archives of life, not like someone from today's world. You look like a museum exhibit, Anatoly Sergeyevich! C'mon, drink this vodka and loosen up. Hey Nadya, give Tolya a kiss. Our birthday boy hasn't been kissed by a woman for decades!"

Nadia, a pretty brunette, went up to Anatoly and landed a passionate kiss smack on his lips.

"Now he's coming back to life, I can see it," said Lev. "Look at him, he's changing trains."

"Hey, we want to change trains too!" someone else shouted.

"Nadia, Nadia, Nadia," others started chanting.

"That's quite a lot of train changes. Our country is poor. Our railway system is no good."

Everyone burst into laughter. Anatoly took a glass of vodka, stood up, and people stopped talking to listen to him.

"How about this one? A man creates a hero's shrine in his house and starts worshipping it. He makes sacrifices, buys expensive ornaments and gifts for the shrine. One day, God comes to him and says: 'Hey you, stop spending everything. If you become poor, you're going to put the blame on me.'"

"That's not yours, Tolya," said Lev. "That's Aesop's. But who cares? Aesop knew more about survival than anyone."

"You people are losing your minds!" somebody shouted.

"They'll squander the fortunes of our country and one day we are going to become a bankrupt state!" somebody else called out.

"Good," said Lev. "Maybe then we can start again and make a better country. Let's drink to Aesop, our brother in slavery."

APPARENTLY EVERYONE AT the party was drunk and laughing, except Vasya, who was only pretending to be drunk. Exploiting the happy distractions, he feigned dropping a glass on the floor and briskly crawled under the table toward me. Shielded from view by the long table cloth, he located my legs. Vasya pulled a small sheet of paper out of his pocket, folded it ever so carefully and waited. Then when I stretched out my left leg, I felt Vasya silently grabbing my shoe and holding my ankle with his cold, sweaty hand. Quickly, he placed the folded piece of paper inside my sock and let go of my leg. I froze as if a bolt of electricity had run up my spine. Lev must have been watching me closely because that was his cue to lean toward me and whisper quietly into my ear.

"Luke, those are the names you wanted. Anatoly gave them to us."

I looked around apprehensively. At the next table, a group of men in dark suits were watching everyone at our table, surveying our party with palpable curiosity. Acknowledging their presence, I pretended to smile back at the men as Lev again whispered in my ear.

"I'm sure those people are *Gebeshniki*.[6] KGB is written all over their faces. Guard that paper well, my friend. If they find it, all of us are dead."

Suddenly Lev yelled out:

"Who wants another drink?"

---

[6] Acronym given to KGB officers.

"A double shot for me, please," called out Vasya, suddenly popping up across the table as if appearing out of nowhere. I noticed Lev, Vasya and Anatoly exchanging a secret glance.

"Come on!" Lev yelled at the waiters. "Serve some drinks to the hardest working men in all of Russia!"

As another bottle of vodka was brought out, Vasya continued chain-drinking out of fear. Lev leaned over to me again and whispered:

"If something goes wrong, we will both die. But we will never rat on you. Okay? So do not worry. You must do the same. Guard the paper well!"

I laughed and nodded at him like I had just heard the funniest joke in the world. Vasya turned to the revelers again, raising his glass.

"Happy birthday, Anatoly Sergeyevich! Happy birthday, you fucking Einstein!"

Vasya looked around the table but couldn't spot Anatoly.

"Where's that museum exhibit? And where's that whore? I only asked her to kiss him! Where'd he run off with her?"

More raucous laughter.

"Now I know why he's so dressed up!"

I GOT UP and strolled slowly to the men's room so as not to attract any attention. Once there, I went into a toilet stall and locked the door behind me. Without pulling down my pants, I sat down on the toilet cover and carefully reached down, found the folded paper in my sock, and pulled it out.

Unfolding the little piece of paper, I found a list of scribbled names in English in tiny print. Weird-sounding names. Important names. Names of the brave people who were standing up against the Communist regime.

My heart started throbbing inside my throat. One glance at that list made it clear that there was no way in hell I could memorize all those names. I took out the pocket knife I always carried with me and cut a tiny slit between the heel and the sole of my right boot. Inside that slit, I carefully folded and placed the list.

Suddenly I heard Vasya walking into the men's room. He was very drunk and humming some Russian song as he started unzipping his trousers. Without making a sound, I remained motionless inside the toilet stall.

Abruptly, the door to the men's room burst open and that group of suspicious men in dark suits walked in. They grabbed Vasya and shoved his head down inside the urinal. Mortified, Vasya started wailing for help.

"Hey! I've done nothing!" he yelled breathlessly. "Please stop! You're hurting me! I swear, I have done nothing wrong! Help!"

I stood up, flushed the toilet and stepped out of the stall. Seeing me, the men stopped in their tracks, but still clutched onto Vasya.

"Let him go," I said to them calmly.

They were looking at one another, not knowing how to proceed. Their leader stood firm, glaring at me but befuddled. I moved toward him casually. Clutching my unopened pocket knife in my fist for ballast, I took advantage of their paralysis by swinging a sharp uppercut at the leader's jaw. It connected and dropped him to the floor, blood oozing from his mouth.

"I'm just a tourist here," I said calmly, rubbing my sore knuckles. "But I did some boxing in my country. So let that man go or else I'll waste more of your fucking faces."

Flabbergasted, the men let Vasya go. He straightened up, moaning softly, and tried to smooth out his rumpled suit.

"I'm making calls about your conduct" I said to them, "to the United States Embassy, to the Human Watch Center in Helsinki and to my lawyer in Geneva."

I could see that their leader's bloodthirsty eyes couldn't focus yet. My punch had surprised him. When he stood back up, he was rubbing his bleeding mouth. He tried barking back at me like a bulldog though some of the aggression had been knocked out of him.

"That man is a criminal! Our conduct is none of your business!"

"He's not a criminal," I said. "You're hurting him just because he was having a drink with me. You need to let him go. I have no doubt you have the wrong person. C'mon, let him go."

Somehow my calm voice seemed to have a soothing effect on their leader.

"OK, Mr. American, maybe it's a case of mistaken identity or maybe it's not. But I will let him go this time. And see, I'm not hitting you back!"

"Thank you and please accept my apologies. Now can you please let Vasily go?"

"Verbitsky, it's your lucky day, you can go now! We'll see you soon, Mr. American."

The leader turned, barked out a command in Russian, and left with the other men.

"You okay?" I asked Vasya.

He stared at me in shock, not knowing how to answer.

"Vasya, are you okay?" I repeated. "Come over here. Let me help clean you up."

I soaked some paper towels in cold water and applied them to the bruise on his face and the scrape on his forehead. His hands were still shaking. I put some hand soap on his head and started washing off the filth from the urinal.

"You saved my life. Those sons-of-bitches would have killed me if you weren't here."

"For a moment, I thought they wouldn't stop. I thought they'd beat me up with you."

"It was funny the way you said you were calling the American Embassy?"

"It sounded good, right?"

"But Helsinki and Geneva? Also just good names?"

"Yeah. I could have added that I was calling my mother in Paris because she's French."

"Next time, Luke, you should also add the United Nations. For some reason, they're afraid of the United Nations."

"Me too, I'm afraid of the United Nations. For good and bad reasons. Everyone should be."

"You're good, Luke. You're very, very good," said Vasya. Then he went quiet. Despite the small talk, I could see his eyes were drowning layer by layer in fear.

"I don't want to leave this bathroom," he announced.

"Listen, Vasya, I'm going to take you home and stay with your family tonight. No one will dare touch you, I promise. I will use scary names like UNESCO if you want, okay?"

Suddenly, a ray of relief appeared on Vasya's face.

"I'm glad that after all this, you can still be funny. But what about tomorrow night? What about then? What's going to happen tomorrow night?"

"Hey, you want me to move in with your family? You've got two rooms, and four people sleeping there already, no? Where do you want me to stay?"

"We have an armchair-bed in the kitchen."

"Okay, okay. I'll stay as long as you can tolerate me."

"You're a good man. Maybe you're American after all."

"What did you think I was?"

"Sorry, I don't trust anybody. But you Americans trust people because your people are free."

"Free for now. Know what Jefferson said? 'The tree of liberty must be refreshed from time to time with the blood of patriots and tyrants.'"

Vasya's eyes opened wide and he glanced worriedly at the door to the men's room, as if the men were just outside listening to us. I understood his concern.

"You mean the rock 'n roll musician, right?"

"Yeah," I said loudly, "that guy from Jefferson Airplane!"

We wanted to make sure that anyone spying on us could not associate Vasya Verbitsky with one of the founding fathers of the United States.

"I love rock 'n roll!" concluded Vasya.

"Yeah, me too!"

"I don't know how to thank you," he said softly. "Can I hug you?"

"Sure."

Vasya put his arms around me and whispered in my ear:

"Do you want to eat some good chicken?"

"Yes," I said, "I'm sick of hot dogs and borsch."

"Let's get some home-made vodka on our way."

"You people ..."

"We'll take the bus. It's safer with people around."

23

WE STOPPED AT a *Prodoukti magazin*[7]. It was full of elderly people. At the *Vino-Vodochni*[8], after standing in the line of shoppers for a long time, we finally reached the check-out register. The bored sales clerk looked too young to be working the evening shift. Vasya said to her:

"Two bottles of *Moskovskaya* and one that's not *Moskovskaya*, please."

The sales clerk understood Vasya's code language. She rang up two bottles of *Moskovskaya* vodka and one bottle of something that looked like water in a milk bottle.

"It's the best *samagon* in town," said Vasya confidentially.

"What's *samagon*?" I asked, keeping my voice low too.

"You'll find out soon enough."

"No, I won't! Home-made vodka, may I presume?

"It's brewed mostly in basements," whispered Vasya, "from beet-root, corn and potatoes. Up to 60 percent of atomic strength alcohol. It's pure health. It disinfects your entire body.

"Don't they sell whiskey here? Scotch?"

Suddenly, everyone in line was staring at me.

"It's better if we don't speak a foreign language in public places," said Vasya.

"Why?"

"They have people everywhere."

---

[7] Grocery shop.
[8] Alcoholic beverage section.

"Who? The KGB?"

"Finally, you're catching on."

We walked out of the supermarket and along Leningrad's deserted, nighttime streets and canals with me trying to keep pace with Vasya. It was freezing cold but strangely beautiful. I could barely keep up.

"Hey, Vasya, who doesn't work for the KGB here?"

"Very good question," he said. "My wife doesn't."

"What about Lev?"

"He's good too. Anatoly as well. But that's as far as I can go."

"What about that old *baboushka* crossing the road?"

"I wouldn't trust her."

"You can't be serious?"

Vasya stopped abruptly and turned to look at me, astonished at my ignorance, his eyes full of sadness.

"Here we live like frightened animals in the zoo, my friend. Have you ever seen the faces of animals in the zoo? They look terrified, unnatural, full of apathy. And worst of all, they know they're condemned to being locked up forever.

"Now look around. Do you see one happy face anywhere on this street? Everyone lives wrapped up in his or her own nightmare of fears. In the zoo, each group of animals thinks that their cage is the best protection they've got against their neighbors and the rest of the world. They feel falsely safe in their cage. They love their cage, their prison. You understand? They'll do anything to keep their prison intact. Because through careful intimidation and brainwashing, through terror and fear-mongering, you can make anyone love his own prison and rat on his neighbors.

"How do you like that for a country to live in? Do you want to raise your family in a zoo? We are modern-day slaves. We live in apartments that the government has built for us, we work at jobs that the government has invented for us. We eat food that the government has provided for us. We travel only where the government allows us to go. We say things only that the government likes us to say.

"Who runs the government? The Communist Party and their Pretorian Guard: the KGB. The KGB will assassinate anyone who is critical of the government. We have no private property, no individual rights, no functioning constitution, no independent judiciary, no freedom of speech and no freedom of movement.

"This is an empire that is based on a vertical power structure. And that structure is operational only when built on lies. So each layer of the society has to lie bigger to advance higher. You have to lie and listen to others lying all the time. Our teachers lie, our historians lie, our politicians, artists and economists lie, and finally these lies permeate your family. They are absorbed into your DNA. And that's what I'm most terrified of.

"I don't want my son to lie. I really don't! There's something awful and humiliating in all of this lying. It eats up one's soul and turns us into pitiful and bitter creatures. You become Lenin's invention, the new Soviet man, a *homo sovieticus*. That's who I have around me here. That's the kind of a country I'm leaving to my son. I'm utterly disappointed in myself and in my generation. It's a generation of brainwashed, frightened people. And I'm one of them."

"No, you're not," I said quietly to Vasya, holding his arm and walking along with him through the silence on that deserted street.

We passed an apartment building where a gigantic poster had been plastered on the corner brick wall portraying Marx, Engels and Lenin together. Vasya paused.

"See those three?" he said. "They're the directors of our zoo. Every time I pass by this poster, I feel like burning that building down."

"You should lower your voice," I told him. "Someone might hear you."

"See, you're here only for a few days and you're already frightened."

"I have to admit this place is scary. Especially at night."

"It's not the place and it's not the people," said Vasya, shaking a finger at me. "It's the system, Luke. The Communist system turns humans into animals in a zoo. We need a revolution here."

"Another one?"

24

FINALLY WE GOT to Vasya's apartment. After greetings and introductions to Marina, Vasya's wife, we found ourselves around the kitchen table practicing the national pastime. Marina asked us to keep our voices down because their son Andrey was asleep in the next room.

"A friend of mine," said Vasya, taking another drink of vodka, "makes a dish with two big melons at the center. You know what the dish is called? 'Reagan's Balls.'"

"I see you have an underground Reagan cult here."

"We love his balls. He has big balls. When he was in Berlin and said, 'Mr. Gorbachev, tear down this wall,' I was laughing so hard. The fucking Russian communists didn't know how to answer him. They were scared. Ha! I loved him so much. For us, Reagan was a good guy. He demanded that they tear down the barbed wire that separated liberty from slavery. Oh God, will I ever see that day? When I finally saw Reagan in a Hollywood film, I was confused. He was a good actor. Was he acting about the Berlin wall too?"

"No, I think at that moment, he meant it."

Relieved, Vasya stared into my eyes.

"I thought so. We can't lose our hope in America, you know. It'll be the end."

I looked at all the empty vodka bottles in disbelief.

"You people are crazy."

"Drink, Luke, drink. You think too much. Tell us, are you married? Do you have a girlfriend? Tell us about your exciting international love life."

"What love life? I'm so far away from all that now."

"Luke, screw the politics," said Vasya. "We can't change anything anyway. We do a few things here and there just to make us feel good about ourselves. Here take a look at this."

Vasya handed me a yellow piece of newspaper from some publication.

"*The Chronicle of Current Events.* The only *samizdat* periodical in the history of the USSR, the only true source of information. The rest of Soviet news publications all have fabricated news. This periodical has been around for 15 years. It has covered all political trials, but not one of the accused has ever been acquitted. We had to close it down in 1983. KGB got on our trail and confiscated the last issue."

"You're too loud again, Vasya" said Marina.

"Why don't you put on the *Machina Vremni*[9] and make it a bit loud." Vasya turned to me. "It's my favorite local rock band. You'll like it, I'm sure."

"Listen, Vasya," I said to change the subject. "If I was going to come to your house, then why'd you crawl underneath the table at the party with the list? You could've given it to me here."

"Is that what Vasya did?" asked Marina. "He crawled under the table and passed you the list?"

"Yes."

Suddenly Marina burst into irrepressible laughter, an awkward, very masculine, misplaced laughter. Nevertheless, Vasya and I hopped on her sudden joyride and started laughing as well.

"We never thought you'd dare come to my place."

"Why not?" I asked, still laughing. "What are they going do to me?"

Marina's laughter swiftly turned into uncontrollable crying. With a worried look, Vasya took her hand and watched her silently.

"I'm afraid," said Marina, still crying. "Just afraid, I'm sorry."

Vasya shook his head silently, picked up the telephone receiver, unscrewed the plastic cap and pulled out a tiny device.

---

9   Time Machine, a famous rock band in USSR.

"Mashka, nothing to worry about anymore. Look, I dismantled it. No one can hear us."

Marina turned down the rock music that had been playing to conceal our words.

"Wait a minute," I said. "Were they listening to us?

"Oh, man, don't be so naive. They can do anything they want to you. You think there are no foreigners who have disappeared here? You have to be careful and you have to keep an eye out all the time."

"Even those old baboushkas who work for KGB?"

"Yes, the ones who sing *Step da Step Krougom*[10], even they can make you disappear."

"Is that why you all drink so much?"

"No, it's because the stock market is fluctuating."

We all broke into laughter again. I don't know whether it was because I was getting scared as well or whether this goddamn Russian *samagon* that Vasya has been pouring into me had eradicated any remaining molecules of resistance. What can you expect from a drink made out of corn and potatoes that is 60 percent alcohol?

"Mashka, stop the music and turn the TV on, I don't want the neighbors hearing us having fun."

Marina switched on the *Vremya* news program where the announcer was declaring the latest achievements in Soviet agriculture and metallurgy.

"More lies?" I asked.

"Yes, but it doesn't matter, my friend. In a few years time, we are going to have Communism here with no borders, no nationalities, no religions, everything will be free, no one will need to work anymore, everyone will be happy, you can come and visit us anytime, except when we are traveling…"

Vasya looked at his wife playfully.

"Where do you want to go on vacation, Marina? After the world revolution, international communism will rule over the planet Earth, and I can take you wherever you want. Paris? No problem."

---

10   Russian folk song.

Vasya pointed proudly at a framed portrait on the wall above the fridge between the kitchen cabinets, which I discovered was none other than Thomas Jefferson.

"Speaking about Paris, don't you recognize your own ambassador to France? Now look at the name at the bottom. Read it aloud."

I stood up and looked closer at the portrait of Jefferson.

"It says 'Eric Von Stonmayer.' Why?"

"So when the KGB comes for their normal *obisk*,[11] I can tell them he's an 18ᵗʰ century German baroque composer."

"Baroque composer? That's smart."

"See how I learned to lie?"

"I better learn to lie too, and fast, right?"

"No," said Vasya. "Please not you."

---

[11] House Search.

25

VASYA GRABBED MY hand and looked straight into my eyes.

"Thank you for standing up for me. It has never happened before."

He hugged me hard.

"No one has ever stood up for me against the authorities. You know, everyone is scared. Including me."

"I understand. This is George Orwell's "1984" in real life."

"Exactly. Government lies to you, tortures and humiliates you like a slave for so long that you become one."

"You're not a slave, Vasya. You're a great man. I admire you."

"Thank you for giving me back my dignity. Now I'm not afraid anymore."

"You think they will leave you alone now?"

"Never! But now I'm not frightened anymore. Maybe for the first time in my life. Can I give you another hug?"

"Sure."

"Marina, my wife, also wants to give you a kiss. I told her what happened."

Suddenly, the entire family was in the room, Vasya's son, Andrey, strolled in wearing pajamas. A little old lady in a pink robe was right behind the boy. Vasya directed Andrey to give me a kiss. The boy did as instructed.

"Grandma too," he said.

The old lady gently kissed my forehead and made a little speech in Russian which Vasya translated simultaneously as she spoke:

"Comrade American, this Communist occupation is temporary. We will gain our freedom back. Sooner or later."

Grandma punctuated the end of her speech with another kiss on my forehead.

"She's the optimist in the family," explained Vasya. "She fought in the Great Patriotic War, maybe that's why. But then Comrade Stalin sent her to a Gulag camp in Siberia just because she was a POW for two months."

Turning to Andrey, Vasya said: "Hey, family, it's time to really go to bed now."

He whispered to me, "Let's put Andryousha to sleep together."

What they called a bedroom turned out to be a tiny space not much larger than a closet, barely habitable for one child. Andrey's tiny bed, a turntable, and a miniature table lamp filled the space to capacity. Vasya covered Andrey with a blanket, tucked him in and kissed him on both cheeks. When Andrey closed her eyes peacefully, Vasya looked over at me with an excited expression.

"Check this out."

He pulled out what looked like a round X-Ray film.

"What's that?"

"An LP."

"LP?"

"Yes, a friend of ours who works in a clinic figured out how to manufacture LPs. He makes bootleg LPs out of x-ray film. You know, Luke, no western music was ever allowed into the USSR. So for Soviet people, there has never been a Rolling Stones, a Jimi Hendrix, a Led Zeppelin, a Deep Purple, not even an Elton John. So my friend decided to manufacture LPs himself. You want to hear it? This one is made especially for Andrey. You'll see what I mean."

Vasya's hands were shaking, but he managed to place the x-ray/LP on the turntable and started it spinning. Slowly, almost painfully, tinny music started to come out of the speakers. It was Billy Joel's "Honesty", played as an instrumental on some sort of toy piano.

"I put my boy to sleep with 'Honesty,' it's his lullaby" says Vasya proudly. "I love Billy Joel. That's Marina playing. She's a cellist, but she plays all kinds of instruments."

After the first verse, Vasya started softly singing the lyrics of the chorus to his little boy:

Honesty is such a lonely word,
Everyone is so untrue,
Honesty is hardly ever heard,
And mostly what I need from you.

Vasya turned back to me. "See, my friend, not everyone is a liar. There are no lies in my family. Entire nation minus one is not an entire nation."

"You're a brave man, Vasya. Remember Jefferson said, 'When governments fear people, there is liberty. When people fear government, there's tyranny.' As long as mother Russia has sons like you, it has a future."

The little boy was already asleep.

"Luke, I think they've injected me with massive amounts of Haloperidol," said Vasya softly, a note of alarm in his voice. "You know about Haloperidol, the medication?"

"No."

"Last time they put me in *psychushka*[12] instead of jail, a doctor injected me with Haloperidol. I don't remember how many times. He said it was harmless, that it just controlled your mood shifts. But Anatoly's a doctor. You know, the guy on the Past Train at his birthday party? He told me the side effects are Parkinson's. Maybe that's why my hands have started shaking. What'd you think?"

"Those people are animals."

"Do you know that Andropov thought that Solzhenitsyn's exile was successful because he went to the West and shut the fuck up."

"Were you disappointed?"

"Of course I was. I wanted Solzhenitsyn to get out there and mobilize everyone to help us out. More than 80% of our young people are listening to BBC and Voice of America. More of you should

---

[12] A mental institution.

come here and publish articles about the brutality of the Soviet regime. Nixon gave Romania most favorite nation status. Why?"

"He did?"

"Politics. Real politics. It's the worst kind. But do you know how lucky I feel now, having you sitting here on the floor of my apartment and giving a damn? Can I share some reading material with you?"

"Of course."

He reached under Andrey's bed and pulled out a well-worn book from underneath, then silently handed it to me. Its cover had been repaired so many times the title was unidentifiable from the outside. "'The Power of the Powerless' by Vaclav Havel. Ever read it?"

"No."

"Take it."

"Thank you."

"Can I just very quickly read you a quote from something else? It's by the great Czech writer Joseph Skvorecky from his book 'The Miracle Game':

"'There were two kinds of Christians. Open ones and secret ones. The open ones let themselves be thrown to the wild animals. The secret ones made their sacrifices to the Roman gods during the day and at night they went to communion. The ones who were devoured became saints. The secret ones survived and spread the teachings of Christ.'"

"Which ones do you think we are here, the open ones or the secret ones?"

"Stay secret. I don't want anything to happen to you."

All of a sudden Vasya's face saddened.

"I'm wondering about that," he said. "Maybe we need the open ones more so people can wake up, no? What do you think?"

"You gave me the list and I have to make it out of this crazy hellhole and get the names published, right? Promise you're going to stay alive.

"Okay, I promise."

We hugged.

"Good night."

81

"*Spokoynoy Nochi.*"

I was walking out of Andrey's bedroom when Vasya stopped me again.

"Hey Luke, take this cassette and listen to it when you get back to the USA."

"What's this?"

"It's *Mashina Vremeni,* Time Machine in English. The best rock band here, the one I told you about."

"Oh, okay."

"We have great rock 'n roll here. You'll see."

"I believe you, Vasya. Good night."

"Hey, Luke, one last thing. Maybe you want to listen to Dean Reed instead? He sings in English."

"No, thanks."

"That's what I thought!" said Vasya. "He was a communist but good person. Yes, it happens sometimes."

We laughed.

26

AS I LAY in the Vasya's armchair-bed in the kitchen, all I could think about was her. It was so narrow that I could only fit into it by lying flat on my back without my arms at my sides. There was no room for my arms. So I crossed them over my chest. It was the closest thing to lying down in a coffin that I had ever experienced.

After that day, chock full of KGB, of lies, of fear and manipulation, of rampant unhappiness, of corruption and horrendous vodka, I was drained completely, searching for a little ray of beauty inside me, something that remained untouchable and pristine.

It was her. My mystery woman. My love. Yes, I had fallen in love with that magnificent creature. Where was she now? I tried to transport myself 5,000 miles back to our first encounter.

After that one time, I went back to The Hole over and over to find her. I'd drink uncountable Holy Grails on every occasion. She never showed up. I asked around. No one knew her. No one ever saw her again. Now during my USSR assignment, she was chasing away the darkness in my brain. Every time I closed my eyes, she would shine her light upon me.

In the Stardust Hotel, we kept kissing each other all night long. My lips were going numb, though she had no intention of stopping. She would just slow down and lick my lips until they'd come back to life. Her lips were full and powerful and they meant business. She was carving passion out of my momentary hesitancy. She would nourish my lips until they were back in full force, and then let me taste her mouth as long as I pleased. Just as I was thinking that we were about finished, she would take me to climb a higher mountain, one that I never knew existed.

When my tongue met her tongue, we froze in ecstasy for a moment. It was a meeting of two wild bees in a flower field. Our mouths were buzzing from the joy of it. Our lips were trembling, singing sounds that I had never heard before. While our tongues were glued together and our fates were being sealed inside our mouths, she grabbed my head and moved it backwards. Then she closed my eyes with her moist palm and urged her nipple inside my mouth, teasing my lips and my tongue, giving in to me playfully.

Oh, God, was this a dream? Did this woman really exist? She gave all of herself to me. All at once. She didn't hold anything back. This was not simply sex. This felt like something sacred. Something divine. Something unspoken and unstoppable, like a great ocean wave breaking against an endless beach.

I'm a man of short sentences. A few clipped words here and there, as needed. "Laconic" is the adjective I would use to describe myself. But during our love-making, I couldn't shut my inner mouth. Unspeakable words were spilling out of my boiling mind. I was afraid that this inner voice would somehow burst out of my mind so that she could hear the madness that I was verbalizing inside. The very thought of that guilelessness was paralyzing.

Like a skydiver plummeting to earth on his first jump, I was free falling in love. I could hardly breathe. She gently pulled her nipple out of my mouth and I slowly opened my eyes. Her bewildered look revealed her own inner tsunami. She lay down next to me. Then she gently put my hands on her lips and burst into a full-hearted cry.

I could tell she was shocked at the feelings that were bouncing around inside her heart. I started to listen closely to her crying. I didn't know that people could talk, even tell stories, through their crying. Gradually her crying expressed real thoughts for me. I understood her entire story, a sad one with many chapters of wrong choices and missed opportunities. It was a cry for love.

Her crying was also our story. She was saying that we were meant for one another. We were manufactured with precision to fit perfectly together. She stopped weeping, and in that silence, we could hear each other's inner voices. There were no human words, just the buzzing of happy bees.

I started kissing her again the way she had taught me to kiss her. This time I was the one taking her for a climb. Her eyes were full of fear and excitement, her lips were dehydrated, her breath got shorter and a little raspy. My mouth went to work, comforting her, moistening her, getting her to relax her breathing, until she fell asleep next to me. Her face was peaceful, a childlike smile hidden behind her sensual lips.

I whispered so softly she couldn't hear me:

"I'm so glad you can't hear me because I can't explain any of my feelings. If you want, we can go to the park tomorrow to play and try to make sense out of all of this. But for now, I love you. Yes, I'm in love with you even though I don't know who you are. It is all so exciting and so daunting. Sleep well, my love. I will cook whatever you want tomorrow morning for breakfast. My name is Luke. Don't forget me. I'll never forget you."

I too fell asleep.

27

MARINA'S SCREAM WAS loud, reverberating throughout the darkened apartment. Startled awake, I squeezed my way out of the armchair-coffin-bed.

"Andrey's got a high fever," said Vasya, looking helpless. His seven-year-old son was shivering under the covers.

"We have to put him in a bath," I said.

"There's no hot water," said Marina.

Seeing my bewildered expression, she clarified:

"Today is Saturday. We get hot water only on Mondays, Wednesdays and Fridays. I'll have Mama make some hot water on the stove."

Marina checked the boy's thermometer again.

"It's too high," she said.

"Can't you call an ambulance?" I asked.

"They take forever to come," said Marina. "We need to do something now. I will call some friends and see who has a fever reducer or an antibiotic."

Marina got on the phone. While she was finding a neighbor who had some medication, Vasya was looking out the front window and down at the street. A black RAF-minivan was parked on the corner. Vasya stared at the vehicle, hesitant and apprehensive.

"Vasya, I'll go and pick up the medicine." I said.

"No, I'll go."

"You stay with Marina and the kid."

"All right. Thank you, my friend. Use the back door."

Marina instructed me on the military-like mission:

"Building 1701, Entrance 3, 4ᵗʰ floor, first apartment on your left. His name is Kolya. He's expecting you."

I grabbed my coat and hurried out. It was a dark, black night. I walked down the empty street lined with Soviet-era, bunker-style apartment towers that were virtually indistinguishable from one another. I almost rushed by my target, but noticed a weather-worn sign for Building 1701 and hurried up to the 4ᵗʰ floor. I knocked on the door of the first apartment on the left and a dog started barking behind the door. Abruptly, the door opened just a crack. I saw a sliver of a man's face.

"Are you the English?" said the man.

"No. I'm the American," I said. "Are you Kolya?"

"No, I'm Misha. Kolya is sick. Here's the medication. Goodbye."

"Thank you."

He shut the door abruptly. I went back outside and retraced my steps along the dark, desolate street. Nothing was moving and no one was in sight. When I got to the lone street lamp at the corner of the Vasya's block, I saw three black cars parked near that black minivan, but pressed on anyway. As I moved quickly along the sidewalk to the back of Vasya's building, a dozen men jumped out of nowhere and quickly surrounded me from all sides.

All I knew how to do to defend myself was get into a crouched boxing position. But just as I did, someone ran up behind me and smashed me on the back of my head with a police baton. I hit the ground like a cement block. After that, I didn't remember much, except that all the men started kicking and punching me. I recognized a couple of those guys as the same thugs who had brutalized Vasya in the men's room at the birthday party.

Not a word was spoken as they continued to beat me up. All I could think of was that they were going to kill me if I didn't do something fast and drastic. My head was bleeding, my stomach was aching from their blows. Suddenly I started coughing dramatically and pretended that I was choking on my own blood. They all paused. One of them leaned over me to check on my breathing. I grabbed the guy by his hair and sank my teeth into his ear lobe, biting a piece of it off and spitting it back into his face. His painful, furious scream echoed through the apartment towers. Windows were opened and voices called out from somewhere above me. Some strong hands picked me up and threw me into the back of the black minivan. Just before I lost consciousness, I remembered being bounced around as the minivan raced through Leningrad's pockmarked streets.

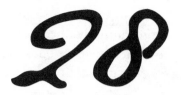

NEXT THING I recall, I was opening my eyes in a big empty room with grey walls and large pictures of Dzerzhinsky, Lenin and Andropov. I was wearing nothing but my underwear, sitting on a cold metal folding chair with my hands tied tightly behind my back.

The first thought that came to my mind was that Vasya was right, that these murderous people were going to eliminate me. I tried to re-focus my eyes and then saw that there was a man with gray hair dressed in a KGB uniform directly in front of me behind a big desk. Seeing the executive chair he was sitting in and the regal way he was drinking tea, I assumed he must have been the guy in charge.

"Good morning, Mr. Forsythe," he said. "Do you want to place a call to the United Nations in Geneva or in Helsinki?"

I couldn't get more than a moan out of my swollen mouth. I heard some men's laughter in the background. Then suddenly a number of men were beating me all over again with their fists, their boots and their clubs. I lost consciousness once more.

How much time went by until my next conscious moment?

It was hard to say because they must have drugged me to flush out all resistance. When I next opened my eyes, I was lying in the big iron scoop of a gigantic yellow bulldozer that was trundling along through rocky countryside. My hands were still tied behind my back and they had put me in some kind of big potato sack. My first thought was, "Okay, I understand, now they're going to dig a hole and bury me alive with a lot of other trash."

But the bulldozer stopped and its massive hydraulic arms started moving the big scoop – with me in it – up towards the grey skies, then forward to the full extent of its reach. There were voices and laughter, gears shifting and some grinding noise. Then the bull-dozer abruptly tilted its scoop and dumped me on the other side of a barbed wire fence onto some cold hard ground.

Lying motionless, I could barely open my swollen eyes, but I was alive. The bulldozer engine was shifted to idle while the voices backed off. What I would discover later was that they had dumped me on the border with eastern Europe between Serbia and Romania, about 900 miles away from Vasya's residential neighborhood in Leningrad where they had picked me up. They must have flown me there in a military helicopter. I guess they wanted to make it an unforgettable experience.

Now a man appeared on the Romanian side of the barbed wire fence, a man I had seen once before in the bathroom in Leningrad assaulting Vasya. He threw my clothes and my boots over the fence. Then the man crouched down and brought his face as close as he could to the fence, almost pressing his nasty brow against it. He spoke slowly in an angry voice, as if he were spitting the words at me:

"You see, Mr. Luke Forsythe, we didn't kill you. But I swear on the prosperity of my motherland, if you ever return to our country, I will have to cut you up and mail the pieces back to your family. Do you hear me, you scum? Nod your capitalistic filthy head if you can hear me!

I managed to move my head a little.

"Let us live in peace," he said. "Mind your own godforsaken business! This is our land, not yours. Welter-weight boxing cham-pion, bullshit! You are a lawyer, some kind of self-proclaimed Robin Hood. But you met the wrong sheriff this time! I will cut your balls off next time, I promise you!"

The man stood up and I heard him marching away. Car doors slammed, a vehicle sped off and the drone of the bulldozer slowly receded. The first thing I did was reach for my boots and pull them closer to my face. I had just enough strength to pull open the heel on my right boot.

Yes! There it was! The goddamned list of political prisoners! With whatever muscles in my jaw that were still working, I smiled.

It was a hard-earned smile that almost cost me my life. Never in my life had I smiled with so much pleasure and pain. From the outside, it probably didn't look like much of a smile because I was half-dead, bruised everywhere and in unqualified pain. Nevertheless, it was a totally joyful smile.

In the distance, I could just make out the bulldozer driving away. With all my strength and determination, I tried raising the middle finger on my right hand in the universal gesture of revulsion. It was for all those repressed people living under totalitarianism everywhere and in solidarity with the unbreakable, outraged spirits of all the Vasyas and Levs in Russia and around the world.

But I could no longer shoot the finger because my finger was broken and seemingly disconnected from my control. I could barely wiggle it much less straighten it up in defiance. So I shot the finger figuratively with the only insulting words that came to my muddled mind:

"Fuck you, Lenin!"

Then I closed my eyes and blacked out.

29

WHEN I NEXT opened my eyes, it was late afternoon. All around me, some sheep with ferocious appetites were grazing on whatever grass they could find. Somewhere a dog was barking. Mladko, the young Serbian shepherd who found me, had a beautiful young wife named Anya who was so pregnant it looked like her belly was about to burst. Fortunately, Anya was a nurse working at the local village clinic. That's where they took me to bandage up my head, my face and my shoulder and put my broken arm in a cast. When they finished bandaging me, only my eyes, my mouth and part of my nose could be seen. Gradually over the next few weeks, I recovered, thanks to this wonderful couple who took care of me like family.

One day in the beginning of my convalescence, Anya was spoon-feeding me in the clinic. I could string a few words together, but my mouth still ached. The shepherd came by for a visit. In his special English, Mladko asked me:

"Which country you from?"

"U.S.," I murmured.

Mladko turned to his wife and explained:

"He's American shepherd. They call them 'cowboys' over there." Mladko turned back to me. "Who could imagine that we'd ever come across a cowboy. You lost your sheep and ended up with KGB, in hands of Romanian Securitate, right? Nothing to do with politics?"

I shook my head disgustedly, but no words came out.

"Don't worry, my friend, we will take care of you. You're safe here. We own the mountains. No one can find you here. Do you know where you are?"

"Yugoslavia?" I barely managed to say.

"Good knowledge of geography. This is Serbia, greatest country on Earth. Good people. Good food. Beautiful women. What else does anyone need, right?

"Freedom?" I asked.

"Freedom is a state of mind, my friend. Here, drink this wine." Anya gave her husband a disapproving look, but didn't interfere when Mladko put the glass of dark red liquid to my lips. The wine burned my throat, but I gulped a little gratefully.

"Can't thank you enough," I forced from my lips.

"Thank Bucefalus, not us."

"Who?"

"That is name of sheep that found you. I call him Bucefalus after Alexander the Great's horse."

They brought me to their home ten days later and I curled up in the bed Anya had prepared for me by their fireplace. The days folded into nights as I slept most of the time. Anya disappeared for a few days and returned with a beautiful little boy she'd given birth to at the clinic. I was soon able to sit at their table and eat meals with them like a real human being. Anya was a wonderful cook. The food they ate was farm-fresh and tasty.

One morning a week later, Mladko and Anya found me smoking a cigarette by the barn where the sheep were milling about.

"Is there something wrong," I asked.

"Nothing at all, Luke," the shepherd explained. "But Anya and I have been talking all week about who's going to be our son's godfather. God sent you to us. So now, with God's blessing, we want to ask you to do us the honor of being the godfather to our son."

"Me? A godfather?" I said. "Believe me, Mladko, you don't want me as your son's godfather. You don't know me. There's a secret that I would like to share it with you: I'm an immoral human being. I'm a drunkard and I like women. Someway, somehow I am sure I commit sins every day. I don't even remember the last time I was in a church. I'm a terrible family man."

"It's all good, Luke," said Mladko. "I was like you before I met Anya."

The baptism ceremony in the thousand-year old village church was perfect. Anya had cleaned my pants and boots and Mladko had lent me one of his nicest shirts for the occasion. The priest motioned for me to pick up my new godson, Kristijan. The holy water was gently poured over the baby's head and the infant cried out his surprise and displeasure. That's when Mladko whispered into my ear:

"It's a re-birth for both of you."

The party in Mladko and Anya's garden was delightful. It was a beautiful afternoon, there was plenty of wine and roast lamb and someone played the *tambura*, casting a magic spell over the proceedings. The villagers danced. For the first time in a long while, I felt alive, really alive.

The music was so contagious even the shepherd and his wife danced. Afterwards, they came over to me and put their arms around me to show their appreciation.

"Mladko and Anya," I said, "I don't know how to thank you for everything. But I have to leave soon."

"We know it's time," said Mladko. "But we want to thank you for joining our family. Let's dance one last time. Together."

30

I OPENED MY eyes. The train I was riding on was running along tracks through urban areas in the northeast corridor of the States. Suddenly in the distance, a large bay of water came into view. I could feel the weight of Chesapeake Bay and the ocean beyond on my shoulders. So much had happened. I hadn't had the time to digest it all and make sense of it. And now, I could see my bandaged face in the flickering reflection of the Amtrak window, alternating between glimpses of the bay. I was a ghost of myself, a sad reminder of the good people I had left behind.

Next to me sat Nicholas Cooper. He was tall, with blond hair and a funny-looking face, a little like a clown. You'd never know on first sight that he was the fiercest lawyer in human rights. He was the reason why I got involved with the Russian project in the first place.

Nicholas kept staring at the crumpled list of Russian dissidents that I had given him. When he glanced up at me, his eyes were full of sincere admiration.

"You did it, you son-of-a-bitch," he said, "You did it!" He continued talking as if to himself. "It doesn't look like much, does it? You'd never know that lives depend on it. I'm so very proud of you, Luke. We all are."

Nicholas meant what he said. He was passionate about what he did and about what I did. But I didn't feel the same pride that he was feeling. Far from it. Actually, I felt really bad because I had left my friends back in that hellhole prison land called communism. What was there to be proud of? I felt terrible and not because of any of the aches and pains from all the bruises and broken bones.

I went back in my mind to a conversation I had had with Marina in Leningrad. She told me that we never think that bad things can happen to us. As a result, we were always unprepared when they do happen. When bad things happen, she said, we waste a lot of life denying it. Then we waste even more of life saying, why did this bad thing happen to me, as if anyone else's suffering could be justified. Then we waste another chunk of life saying it can't be that bad. Still another big portion of life is shoved down the sewer when we say it's bad but it'll get better. And when that doesn't work either, Marina continued, only then do we say, okay it's bad and most likely it'll get worse unless I move my ass right now and do something about it.

"By this time," Vasya jumped in, "you're in the hands of God, or fate, or destiny or worst of all, blind chance."

Marina asked me, "Where does all this unfounded optimism come from?"

Before I had an opportunity to respond, she continued:

"You know, Luke, you're the American here. After all, isn't America the land of boundless optimism? Maybe it's your inherent belief in goodness? The primordial American vision of life? Or is it a simple act of self-preservation, maybe even naive stupidity?"

"Who wants more vodka?" injected Vasya.

"I have to be honest," I said. "I no longer know what I think. And that's the truth."

"Here's what I think. It's love," Marina said. "It's love that makes us good. It's love that makes us believe in goodness and compels us to make sacrifices. It's love that gives meaning to human existence. Nothing else. You can claim, 'I'm alive only when I love.' Otherwise, you're like a blind corpse waiting for your own autopsy."

"Blind corpse!" said Vasya, bursting into laughter. "My wife has quite the imagination, no?"

"Love is all kinds of loves," Marina continued. "Love for your kids. Love for your parents. For your woman. For your man. Just love. You can love a tree if you want, and soon you'll see that same tree rewarding you with fruits and scents. You can love a stone, too. And you'll see that very stone caressing your hand when you touch it. Just love."

Marina turned to Vasya and continued, "This is something I have wanted to say to you for a long time. Somehow these words were stuck in my chest and now they just came out."

Vasya grabbed Marina's hand and gently squeezed it.

"I didn't say anything wrong, did I?" said Marina.

"See Luke, see what I mean? We can't even talk about love here without being afraid," concluded Vasya.

31

AFRAID OF LOVE? The thought was a paradox in itself. Isn't love the most desired pursuit that every human being dreams of? Why be afraid of love? Maybe because unlike any other human condition, loving requires you to be naked. To be vulnerable. With no protection at all. And it's tough to be out there unprotected. Someone will prey on your heart and steal it. Guaranteed. Because there are not too many genuine hearts left on our planet Earth. Most of the hearts now on the market are cheap Chinese knock-offs. So Vasya was afraid and rightly so. What about me? Was I afraid too?

"No," I told my inner self.

"Yes," I said back to me.

"Definitely not."

"It's a yes and you know it."

"I don't want to confront this now," I finally murmured to myself. "Maybe just leave me in peace."

As the train pulled into Union Station, I picked up my battered valise and stepped onto the platform. There were crowds of people all over the station, rushing along like a swarm of bees. I felt exhausted, just barely able to stand on my feet. I stopped, dropped my suitcase on the tile floor of the platform in the middle of all that bustling movement and sat down right there. A nearby sign read "NO SMOKING ANYWHERE IN STATION."

I lit up a cigarette just to make sure that I disobeyed all posted rules. Nicholas walked over and looked down at me.

"Are you all right?" I heard his baritone voice say.

"I just need a minute."

"I'm going to make a quick call to my pal at *The Washington Post*," said Nicholas. "We need to get over there as soon as we can and fill them in on the backstory. Will you be okay for a couple minutes?"

"Yeah."

"I know what you need. Black, no sugar, right?"

"Right."

"Don't move."

Nicholas walked away.

All around me, hundreds of feet were passing by. All kinds of feet, running, almost flying. Some were dragging their feet as if their bodies were just too much to bear. And there were the hesitant feet of curious kids being pulled along by their parents. But of course what grabbed my attention out of this fleet of feet sailing along the platform were all the feminine legs. They moved along in short skirts, long skirts, medium-length skirts, bare skinned or with tight-fitting hose. They were softening the air, giving life to this otherwise random flock. Just as my eyes were turning blurry and my usual brain fog was setting in, a remarkable pair of purple shoes paused next to me. I looked up. The purple shoes were accompanied by a yellow dress. And underneath the yellow dress was a sensual shape that spoke volumes to me.

It was her!

"Hey!" I said.

It was too noisy in the station. She didn't hear me. I retracted every single one of my previous undue remarks about God, fate and destiny. Right at that moment, I regained my full faith in all of them. Suddenly I felt blind chance was not as blind as it pretended to be. Because right there and then, what so-called blind chance offered me, the Department of Homeland Security with all its millions of CCTV cameras couldn't accomplish in 100 years.

I took a deep breath and dove into the torrent after her. She floated away from me with a stride that only goddesses could pull off. Wherever they go, they own the place. As I walked some distance behind her, my mind was frantically re-looping the same scenario over and over again. I needed to talk to her. I had to absolutely talk to her. But as the moments passed, fear set in. Would she even remember me?

With my bandaged head, wearing Vasya's worn-out jacket and Mladko's Serbian shirt, I looked more like a migrant worker who's been robbed and pushed around, looking for shelter and a bottle of booze. I was nowhere near looking like the mysterious, arrogant and abrasive drifter that she once was attracted to.

That was me then, and this is me now. How pathetic I must have looked! Would she see that this was the same guy? Because if anything had changed about her, it was that she was more striking than ever, even more beautiful than before. The world must simply bow at her feet. Everyone took notice of her when she walked by. She crossed the gigantic lobby in Union Station and walked straight into the central cafe. I was right behind her and I followed her in. People lined up at the café counter and ordered food and beverages with accents from all over the world. Curiously, only two people were waiting in the line without saying a word. She and I. Then for no reason at all, she turned and looked over her shoulder. Our eyes met but she didn't seem to notice me. She just saw the bandages. Ten seconds later, she looked back at me again, this time very slowly, taking her time to study me more carefully. I tried to smile through my bandaged mouth. Our eyes met again and at that moment she finally recognized me. Her jaw dropped and she gasped for breath like a shock wave had hit her. She covered her mouth with her hand and her face turned into a horror mask.

"Hi," I said.

She turned back around and rapidly walked out of the café, almost running across the main hall of the station. I stood there, stunned like a man who was witnessing his own funeral. I should've waited to speak. I should've said something more. I should've explained better. What was I thinking? What was I expecting? That she was going to put her arms around me? Hug me and love me? Drop her life and follow me anywhere?

How come I understood other people's problems so well? But when it came to taking care of my own shit, I was like those brainwashed Eastern Europeans, indoctrinated to being in my own prison. Or I was like that frightened garage attendant who couldn't show his true feelings to loved ones. Hey, maybe I was the brainwashed, frightened loser, not them. At least they tried. Here, I was walking into black hole after black hole of my own making, cascading from one emotional wreck to another, without ever trying to change things.

32

WHY DID I let her get away? For the first time in my entire life, I was overcome with self-pity. It was an awful feeling. It shrank you to a tiny, bent-over, decrepit version of yourself. Your face turned into the mask of a beggar who was pleading for a piece of his lost dignity. You felt cursed and condemned, robbed of the gifts of life and devoured by indulgence. You wanted to scream. You wanted to whine, "Why me? Why me?"

I picked up the cup of black coffee and drank it like vodka, with one long swallow. It burned my mouth, but I loved the pain and relished the bitter taste of it. I ordered a second cup and drank it the same way. There I was sitting at the café table, feeling sorry for myself and filling up the black hole of my low self-esteem with bitter coffee.

I looked up and I discovered her standing in a far corner of the train station, observing me from a distance like a lepidopterist studying a cocoon that was about to transform into a rare butterfly. Through the bustling crowds, we locked our eyes together almost hypnotically.

PA announcement after announcement came up over the station's loud speaker system as the dispatcher's almost inhuman voice sent travelers to platforms where trains were departing for destinations throughout North America.

Except us.

We were the only two people who were going nowhere, frozen in time. She started slowly walking towards me. Almost reluctantly, she made her way step by step through the throngs of people, disappearing behind the flow of bodies like a phantom, then reappearing, closer and closer. She finally arrived at my café table and studied my bandages for a long moment. She confirmed to herself that it was indeed me.

Abruptly the movie theater in my head was open for business again. What was playing was an old classic in black & white that was starring her and me. Flickering on the screen was a love scene set in a gorgeous railway station with plenty of extras running around. But the movie in my mind suddenly went dark because she sat down at the table and burst into laughter.

I'd heard that laughter before. It was a delightful mix, two parts curiosity and one part fear. It resounded with the joy of discovery, the true music of life. I couldn't take my eyes off of her.

"I didn't expect to see you again," she said.

"I've thought about you every day since then," I said, my voice void of any confidence. A long silence happened naturally.

"It's a miracle that we meet again, don't you think?" I continued with difficulty.

"I just can't believe it," she said. "Look, I don't even know what I'm doing here."

"I understand."

"No, you don't."

"Okay, I don't."

I took all the cash I had in my wallet and put it in front of her on the table.

"I think you forgot this the last time."

"I feel awful about the money. I'm sorry if I offended you."

"Hey, I liked it."

"I'm ashamed and I can't explain."

"I understand."

"No, you don't. But still I can't explain."

"You don't have to. Can I get you something?"

"No thanks. Did you have an accident?"

"Sort of."

"I think I'd better go."

"Wait. Can I see you again?"

She didn't answer.

"We have to meet again. This only comes once in a lifetime. You know it."

"Luke, I'm…"

"You remembered my name?"

"I'm Louisa."

"Nice to see you again, Louisa, Louisa, Louisa," I kept repeating her name.

"Nice to see you, too."

She abruptly stood up, leaving my money on the table.

"I'm leaving for New York today," she finally said after a long pause. "Meet me Friday, say noon, on the corner of 47th and Lexington Avenue?"

"47th and Lex?"

"Yes, at 12 o'clock noon. There's a boutique hotel there I like to stay at."

"Okay. That's great, Louisa."

"See you then, Luke."

She was gone in the blink of an eye. I stood up, overwhelmed by my emotions, almost unable to breathe, trying to follow her with my eyes. But she disappeared too fast. I was still standing there when Nicholas appeared out of nowhere with a cup of coffee in his hand.

"Hey, I was looking for you. I see you got some coffee. Sorry, I was on the phone for a long time. Let's get a cab. They're expecting us at *The Post* right away."

"Hey, Nick…"

"Yes?"

"Never mind. Let's go."

"Just say it. What's on your mind?"

"I was just going to ask you if you believe in destiny."

"Did you get into Dostoyevsky over there?"

"No, I'm getting into Dostoyevsky over here."

Nicholas stared at me with a bewildered look.

"Forget it. I'll tell you the details later."

"One thing is for sure. Someday we have to write a book about all of this."

33

THAT FRIDAY AT noon, I was standing on the windy sidewalk at 47th and Lexington in front of the Roger Smith Hotel. It was chillingly cold. I had spent the entire night chain-smoking and staring at the moon like a lost wolf. I could hardly wait to meet her again. My sleep-deprived body was trembling under my leather jacket. The wounds and the bruises on my face and head were sore and biting into my skin. I had taken off my bandages that night and now my bruises were exposed to the cold Atlantic gusts of Manhattan for the first time.

It was terribly painful, but the adrenalin was kicking me so high that I couldn't feel anything except the heat wave that was running through my blood stream. It turned the warm air coming out of my mouth into a cumulus of curling vapor. It looked like I was shaking from the cold, but my shaking was really due to my heart pounding like a church bell inside my chest.

She arrived an hour late, pulling up to the sidewalk in front of the hotel in a white vintage Corvette with tinted black windows. When she lowered the passenger window to say hello, I barely recognized her. She was wearing large sunglasses and a brown fur coat. Her short skirt exposed those stunning legs just enough to make my mind scream.

I got in and she drove down Lexington toward the Chrysler Building. I said hi. She said hi back. Nothing else. No other words were spoken. No apologies for being late. No, it's cold. No, it was the traffic. No, the weather is vile. No, how was your day. No, thanks for asking, how was yours. None of that crap. She simply looked at me and smiled. And I smiled back at her. And our smiles said it was so great to be together again. Life suddenly seemed easier. Living was light-hearted, more exciting. We continue smiling and that turned into giggling. She was checking out my bruises. I was checking out her movie star sunglasses. We both thought the other looked hilarious.

"I missed you all night long," she said.

"Me too," I replied.

"Suddenly I don't need words to feel comfortable or to hide behind."

"Me neither."

"Want to go somewhere special?"

"Where?"

"Away from all this mayhem."

"Just you and me?"

"Just you and me."

"Does such a place exist?"

"Oh, just wait until you see it."

Our worlds were locked in perfect harmony. I knew it. She knew it too. We both knew it at the same moment. All of a sudden, I wanted to burst out singing. Somehow she read my mind.

"I want to sing too," she said.

I looked at her in awe.

"Isn't that what you were thinking?" she asked.

"It's not safe to think around you."

"No safety at all. There are no barriers in between us. Don't you feel it?"

"I do."

"Are you scared?"

"Sure. It feels like a tsunami is washing me away. I have no more control."

"Oh God, me too," she said, erupting into her sparkling laughter.

She slid a Tears for Fears' CD into the car stereo. "Everybody Wants to Rule the World" cracked through the air. She sang the opening lines along with the recording:

Welcome to your life,
There's no turning back,
Even while we sleep we will find
You acting on your best behavior
Turn your back on mother nature
Everybody wants to rule the world...

I joined her at the chorus and started lip-synching with her, miming, doing moves, pretending I was both the guitarist and the lead singer. I was feeling free and foolish just like when I was a teenager. She laughed again, even louder. Seeing the joy on her face made all my fears vanish. Oh God, I loved being a clown for her! I rested my hand on her thigh. She didn't say anything. She only covered my hand with hers. I leaned over and kissed her hand. She caressed my hair.

We left Manhattan and she was driving fast, way too fast. Faster than my mind was racing along. The Long Island countryside was flying by us. And so were the clouds above. I looked up and saw her dazzling profile eclipsing the afternoon sun. She was as powerful and desirable as a Greek goddess.

Damn, I was already so in love with this woman that I would become a fruit tree for her. I would become a hot stone lying on her back. I would embrace her and have that embrace frozen forever in a stone statue by Rodin. Maybe they'd put our statue in one of those beautiful Parisian parks where people could walk around and look up at us. Lovers would kiss next to us. Kids would play at our feet and elderly people would rest on the bench near the pedestal where we would stand rain or shine, through cold winter days forever warm in each other's embrace.

Suddenly it dawned on me that I was not myself anymore. That I had never truly loved anyone before, despite how much love I'd felt for other women in my life. I had always judged them. I'd felt more trapped than liberated by them. How come now I felt more fulfilled? Some sort of a deep void had been replenished. Trapped, fulfilled, liberated, frightened. How come all these emotions were happening in me at the same time?

Why did I always have an overwhelming need to keep a piece of my own identity free. Unattached to anybody or anything. Free of engagements, commitments and promises. I had never given in all the way. What had I been scared of?

With her, it was different. For the first time in my life, I was hijacked by real love, condemned to live or die in her arms. She looked into my defenseless eyes and read my entire predicament in one glimpse.

34

SHE PARKED THE Corvette by the sea next to an empty stretch of sandy beach near Montauk where an abandoned pier jutted out from the coast into the water. As our bare feet touched the white sand, she started running along the beach, flying like a gazelle. I followed her as best I could. We were moving across the sand like two wild animals tasting their newly found freedom.

She was giggling, laughing, screaming, making all kinds of funny sounds. She invited me, tested me, challenged me. I was running as best I could, but awkwardly, like a flat-footed bear. My body still hurt everywhere, but the pain didn't matter anymore. The only sounds I made were chortles, burps and hisses. She reached the empty pier and climbed up on top of the wooden structure that had been worn down by the salty air. I finally made my way to the pier, and as soon as I climbed up there, she started slowly walking backwards like a cornered deer, teasing me to catch her. I moved toward her step by step because I was completely out of breath after the beach trot. I reached her at the end of the pier, and when I tried to take a deep breath, she kissed me hard and pushed her tongue inside my lips.

Reflections of diffused pink and orange from the setting sun were engulfing the ocean with a blanket of sparkling light. It was a postcard paradise. The last rays of the sun bounced off the water, heating up our bodies and burning our lips. She kissed me differently than before. It wasn't soft nor even gentle. Her arms tightened around my neck and one of her legs wrapped itself around the back of my knee like an octopus trying to squeeze the last breath of life out of me. Her grip was so tight that her strength stunned me. She possessed me totally as I let myself disintegrate in her arms. All the while, her eyes were smiling at me, comforting me, convincing me to let go, to give in all the way.

She went down on her knees and brought me along with her. While still kissing me, she unbuttoned her blouse, then opened my shirt. As her breasts touched my chest, an electrical shock of love surged through our bodies. It must have traveled through the pier and into the ocean because, without any warning, a frothy wave rose up and crashed over the railing, soaking us from head to toe. We trembled from the cold water, we laughed, we squeezed each other even harder and dropped onto the wooden planks as one.

We were kissing and rolling all over the pier and didn't notice or care about the storm that was approaching. Out of nowhere, the wind came up and bigger waves started swelling and breaking against the coast. The setting sun was suddenly smothered by dark clouds that appeared above our heads, leaving us at the mercy of the invading winds that battered the pier. Louisa didn't care about any of it. She kept kissing me, laughing, kissing me more as we were getting soaked from the crashing waves. As the pillars of the pier got pounded by heavier and heavier waves, they started groaning, making a frightful sound. The entire wooden structure vibrated as if it might give way. It didn't scare her in the least. She continued smiling at me, kissing me, loving me.

The pier was swaying so much that I got seasick. Her kisses were unstoppable. I was breathless. A gigantic wave cascaded over the pier and separated us. I was just able to grab the railing which saved me from being washed into the ocean. The same wave pushed her away from me and pinned her down at the end of the pier. We were a good 20 feet apart from each other and the storm was now hammering down on us with all its fury.

"Hey, Luke, come to me," she said.

I was terrified.

"Don't be afraid, Luke," she continued, reassuringly. "Come closer."

Carefully I moved toward her and when I got near, I tried to grab her hand and pull her up to me. But instead, she grabbed my hand and pulled me towards her. The wind was howling madly, battering our faces and whipping her hair around. Still she was unafraid. Her face was calm, determined, serene. She even looked happy being out in the tempest.

She hugged me and started laughing again. Somehow her laughter was louder than the sound of the crashing waves. I had never heard laughter so full of life, so gallant and so desperate all at the same time. She put her head on my chest, kissing my neck, and looked at me in peace.

I felt bigger than the waves, empowered by her fearlessness. We clung to one another at the edge of the pier, kissing as the storm pounded us. I felt her unbreakable spirit as she gazed into my eyes. Amazingly, I was unafraid too. Mesmerized by her courage, I covered her head with uncountable kisses.

The storm seemed to be running out of rage. It moved away from the coast slowly, defeated and humiliated. As quickly as it had appeared, it was gone. And the pink horizon came back again as if nothing had interrupted our paradise.

Exhausted, we rolled onto the wooden deck of the pier. She lay next to me with her eyes closed, moaning about a bruise on her hand. I kissed it and discovered that her hand was soft and fragile. Where did that strength come from? Where did that courage come from? She had helped me to get over my own fears. She had made me brave. Now I was ready to die for her. She opened her eyes and looked at me.

"You're the most handsome man I've ever met."

"Me?"

"Yes, you're absolutely gorgeous."

"Wait a minute."

"I have never said those words to any man in my life."

"Now, you wait a minute."

"I'm so lucky to have you."

"Wait, wait. There's some confusion here. It's me who's lucky, you understand. It's you who's the goddess here."

"Your beauty inspires me."

"What? Oh, God. Me? I'm so … Just look at you. You take my breath away."

"You make me want to scream."

"Scream?"

"Yes, like this!" She screamed.

Her scream scared off all the seagulls that had come to rest on the beach after the storm. The birds took off in terror and she burst into joyful laughter. I joined in with her, unable to say all the things I wanted to say to her. There were so many things that I wanted her to understand.

"Say them. C'mon, speak up! I want to hear them!" she said.

But I couldn't find the words, those traitors. They had betrayed me when I needed them most. All the words had evaporated without warning.

"They left," I told her.

"Who?"

"The words."

She laughed.

"Do you want to know how much I want you?" I asked.

"Yeah."

I climbed up on top of the railing at the end of the pier. I looked at her and jumped over the edge. As I was plunging down into the water, I could see her eyes full of disbelief. The water was stunningly cold. As I came up to the surface, I saw her jump into the ocean not far from me. She popped up, shivering like me. We held each other close and started kissing again with our trembling lips.

35

IT WAS ALREADY dark when we arrived at Martha's Inn, a quaint bed and breakfast on the outskirts of Montauk. Louisa was asleep in the passenger seat. I parked her Corvette near the neon sign that said "Vacancy." Our clothes were still wet. We were cold and exhausted. I rang the antique doorbell on the porch.

"Coming, coming! Wait a minute," called out a forceful female voice with a distinctly eastern European accent.

"Please hurry, we're freezing out here," I said.

A stout middle-aged woman wearing a bathrobe with her hair in curlers opened the door.

"Come in. Welcome! My name is Mrs. Ledowsky, but everyone calls me just Martha. You need a room for tonight?"

"Yes, do you have one available?"

"Are you kidding? This is off-season, we're practically empty. Choose any room you want."

"Look, Martha," I explained in a whisper. "My friend is asleep in the car. I want to get her to the room without disturbing her too much."

Like the experienced hostess that she was, Martha understood the situation immediately and lowered her voice.

"Oh, I apologize, sir. I used to be an opera singer. My vocal chords are naturally strong. But see, I can speak in a whisper too. We won't disturb her, okay?"

"I'd really appreciate it."

As I was guiding Louisa up the stairs, Martha walked in front us with a ring full of keys in her hand. She whispered to me over her shoulder:

"Do you want a room with a view of the garden or of the ocean?"

"The one that has the biggest bathtub."

"That would be the Jasmine Room."

"Thank you."

Martha opened the front door of the Jasmine Room and whispered: "Would you like some hot tea?"

"Yes, please."

"Okay. I will be back in a minute."

I gently lay Louisa on the bed and kissed her moist lips. She opened her eyes a little.

"Make love to me," she said.

"You mean right now?"

"Yes, right now."

"Martha's coming up with hot tea any moment."

"So?"

She slipped off her wet dress in one swift move and lay on the bed in her bra and panties. Her glowing body was radiating desire. Her playful eyes challenged me to act there and then.

"Take it all off," she ordered.

As I try to unhook her bra, she said, "Not that way. Take it off with your teeth."

She sat up on the bed and I went around and tried biting into her bra. No matter what I did, the damned bra didn't budge. I couldn't unfasten it.

"Not that way."

She turned to me and helped me lift the front of the bra with my mouth. As her breasts popped out, she burst into laughter. My awkward moves were hilarious manifestations of my desire for her. She couldn't stop laughing. She stood up.

"Keep going," she said.

I knelt down in front of her, grabbed her panties with my teeth and started pulling them down. But they didn't move. I quickly discovered that, behind her back, she was holding her panties with her free hand. Seeing my helplessness prolonged her laughter. Finally, I figured out her game. Her playfulness and exultation were contagious. I was discovering an anarchistic tribal freedom that was almost Amazonian. I got up and took off all my clothes except my underwear.

"I'm ready."

"Let's run!"

"Run where?"

"To the castle."

"The castle?"

"The one where no one can reach except us. Follow me."

We started running around the room in circles. We jumped on the bed, we jumped off the bed, we got up on the chair, we got down from the chair. I was trying to catch her, and even though she was exhausted, she was always one step ahead of me, giggling all the while.

"I haven't jumped this much since I was in middle school."

"Wait," she said, "it's not finished."

"What else do you want me to do?"

"Let's climb up now."

"What?"

"Up to the top of the castle. To get the magic wand."

She got up on top of the desk. I was one step behind on the chair when Martha knocked on the door. Immediately, we jumped into the bed and covered ourselves with the quilt. Louisa closed her eyes, pretending to be asleep, and buried her head in the pillow.

"Come in, Martha," I said with a tired voice.

Martha quietly entered and carefully placed the tray with teapot and cups on a table. As she was leaving, Martha turned at the doorway and whispered:

"Have a good night. If you need anything else, just dial 9. The phone is always next to me."

"Thanks, I think we'll be just fine," I whispered.

"Yes," she said with a little wink, "I know you will."

As soon as Martha shut the door, Louisa pulled her closed hand out from under the quilt and held it over my head.

"Open it."

"What for?"

"It's the magic wand."

Gently, I opened her hand. Inside were her panties. I felt my heartbeat quicken next to her nakedness. She opened her thighs slightly.

"Touch me," she whispered. "Softly, gently."

I started touching her and her body started moving under the quilt in a slow dance. Her swollen red lips were radiating heat. I started caressing her all over her body with my lips and tongue.

"Luke, how did I ever live without you?"

"Keep talking. I love your lips."

"I love your fingers."

"Oh, Louisa."

"Thank you for being patient with me, Luke. I have waited for you all my life."

"And I've waited for you."

"I'm happy for the first time ever, truly happy. I don't want this moment to end."

We went on kissing and touching, our breathing getting heavier. Our lovemaking was now in full crescendo. Abruptly she grabbed my head and gazed straight into my eyes. Her look penetrated me as she climaxed. She screamed as she came. It was a sound that I had never heard before. It was laughter and weeping mixed with hope and anguish. It was pleasure and pain mixed with gratitude and anger. Exhausted, overwhelmed, burned out like a meteor crashing into the earth, I collapsed next to her.

When I woke up the next day, Louisa was gone. I put my clothes on and hurried downstairs. As soon as Martha saw me, she said, "She took the car and left."

I mumbled to myself, "Again?"

I was speechless, staring at Martha with a vacant look. Finally I asked her, "Did she say anything? Did she leave me a note?"

"Yes, as a matter of fact, she did."

Martha handed me a carefully folded piece of hotel stationery. A telephone number was inscribed on it like figures chiseled into marble on Grant's Tomb. I smiled. Martha smiled too.

"I'll give you a lift to the train station," she said.

36

NOW, 10 YEARS later, here I was driving on Chesapeake Bay Bridge Tunnel in Virginia on the 3rd day of my journey. The rain was still coming down non-stop, a crazy downpour. But it was nothing compared to the storm that was raging inside me. I had driven 438 tortured miles since I'd left Charleston and I had another 481 miles of memories to cover before I would see the love of my life again in Montauk. The ocean on both sides of the bridge was gray and murky, the sky menacing, those Virginia marshlands stretching out and evaporating into the haze. In the back seat, my invisible companions were all silent and scared. Demonic winds from the ocean were vibrating my car.

"Don't be afraid, my love," I heard Louisa's call from the past ringing inside my head just like Calypso's voice. Gods, Odysseus stayed seven years captive to Calypso. She wanted him all to herself until Zeus ordered her to let Odysseus go back to his wife. I've been captive for 10 years now, and I can assure you that I know something that Homer didn't.

My dear poet, did it ever occur to you that maybe Odysseus was in love with Calypso and all this blame aimed at her wasn't justified. Odysseus loved Penelope, too. How can that be, I hear all you thousand-year-olds screaming? He had two hearts! Get it? Unlike all of you and that includes you, my beloved Homer, Odysseus had two hearts and he loved with both, all at the same time. Hey you, mystery crowd occupying the witness stand in my back seat, were you ever going to say anything? Could you put in a word for me to Zeus?

Could he talk to Louisa? Both my hearts were like the ocean on either side of that bridge now, weeping and howling at the same time.

As I tried to catch up with my past, it was playing tricks on me, revealing itself in bits and pieces. The past had a tendency to turn itself into an illusion when we tried to remember it. Many times we invent a convenient past so we could justify our egotistical actions. Not this time, I was thinking, no way. I wanted to know what really happened and how I felt back then, the naked, bare-bone truth, please.

God, I love this woman even more now than I did ten years ago! It's a terrible thing to confess to yourself, but it's true. I remembered that feeling like I was riding on a love balloon, high above the earth, unable to breathe because there was almost no oxygen up there.

After the bridge, there was a rest area and I pulled off the road there. I had to open a window and get some fresh air in my damned car. I let the engine idle as I rolled the window down. The engine sputtered and died. I tried re-starting it without success. All I heard was the grinding sound of the starter and the motor coughing and refusing to kick over.

The rain lessened to a drizzle. I popped the hood open and a geyser of steam rose from the radiator, almost burning my hand. I was stuck there with nothing more than memories searing my heart with painful truths. It was already evening. I walked over to the public bathrooms where a sign told me that I was on Bayside Road, near the town of Exmore, Virginia. The salty rain from the ocean was charged with a fine layer of sand. The few cars that passed me by didn't bother to stop, regardless of how much I waved my arms to get their attention. Standing outside my car in the rain, utterly forsaken by the world, it somehow felt like I deserved all this shit. Then unexpectedly, a strange memory dawned on me.

I could see myself in Martha's car being driven to the Montauk train station that morning 10 years before, so happy, so much in love. I was so absorbed by that vision that I could see myself from outside looking at me through the windshield of Martha's car. I could see the man I was that day, a happy man. I watched Martha's car drive away, taking me and my past with it. I saw my happy self vanishing over the horizon and I was roiled by a wave of desperation. Would I ever be that happy again?

I opened my car door dejectedly, got back into the gloomy driver's seat and dropped my head on the steering wheel in disgust. Then I started banging my head against the steering wheel, every blow reminding me of how much I missed my past self.

37

THE MARTHA'S INN sign gradually disappeared in the good woman's rearview mirror that day a decade ago. Her bed and breakfast, the grounds, parked cars, and racks of surfboards, everything shrank to nothing more than a dot behind me. Then it vanished altogether. Martha was wisely silent as she drove me that next morning to the Montauk station to catch a train back to the city.

Why had Louisa left me again without even a goodbye?

Women. Who can figure them out? They can't even figure themselves out, so what chance do men have? Men and women don't even seem to belong to the same planetary system. Men know more about mountains on the moon or electromagnetic fields on Saturn's rings than they do about the women they share their beds with every single night. They're more in love with the moon or Saturn's rings than with their loved ones.

Not me. I was so in love with Louisa that my heart was on fire. "Stop your car right here," I would have liked to tell Martha, "and let me out near the coast. I'll walk down to the shore and drink up the ocean!" Louisa had given her fire to me. When you have that burning inside, it makes you smile perpetually. Look at me. I couldn't stop smiling. It was almost embarrassing. That damn grin was stuck on my face like glue.

Fire gives birth to new life. It makes you feel so alive. I love the ocean. I love this solitary road skirting the coast of Long Island. I love the clouds that floated above me. I love myself. Yeah, I am a good man. Otherwise, she wouldn't love me so much, right? Right!

Martha slowed the car down to a crawl to pass a group of bicyclists and I felt a familiar salty breeze. Then another unexpected vision came over me. I could see my future self. Clearly I saw myself 10 years in the future, sitting behind the wheel of a broken-down car with marshlands all around me. My future self saw me passing by and gestured frantically for help, begging me to stop. My future self was waving his arms, but everybody ignored him. There I was as we passed my paralyzed car. What I saw was a tired man who had given up and was in the driver's seat banging his head on the steering wheel. That man was lost, without a trace of happiness. He had no more fire inside.

I prayed Martha wouldn't stop her car to help the future me. I didn't want anything to do with that guy. "That couldn't be me," I wanted to scream. I wanted to beg Martha to please not help that hapless driver. Thankfully, she accelerated and drove past the future me. I turned and saw myself fading away through the back window. A flood of relief washed over me. Even though I felt a deep pang of sorrow for the future me, he was on his own as far as I was concerned. He had to learn how to look out for himself. I had my own life now. I wanted to live it to the fullest.

Martha let me out in front of the main entrance of the Montauk train station. She got out of her car and I gave her a big hug goodbye, thanking her for her hospitality. I went inside the station to buy a ticket back to Manhattan.

The middle-aged woman who was working in the ticket booth at the Montauk train station wore a blue cashmere sweater with an open neckline. She leaned forward to hand me my ticket back to Manhattan, and I got a quick glimpse of her generous breasts. They were beautiful and so was she. I looked at her with approval, and she saw the twinkle in my eye. Sensing my appreciation, she blushed. I blushed too. I didn't know what had happened to me, but since I fell in love with Louisa, I was attracted to every woman in the world, no matter their size or shape. I found all the women of the world were now beautiful in their own way.

On the train back to the city, wherever my eyes wandered, I found something sensual about every female passenger who rode in my car. One wore black stockings, her legs a little spread opened.

Another wore red lipstick on her puffy lips, ready to be kissed. Another had hands so tender and gentle that I wanted to hold and caress them. On top of that, I could smell each of their distinct perfumes. Every aroma made every woman seductive in her own way.

From the corners of their eyes, some of the female passengers were also checking me out, either directly or through reflections in the window. For the first time, I could sense their eyes glancing at me and it made me feel embarrassed. I was an intruder in a female realm that didn't belong to me. Yet, I had been briefly invited into that world to look at them, to cherish them and to embrace them, though only in my fantasy.

The train moved along the tracks and I closed my eyes. My Louisa emerged from the darkness. At first I saw her lips in the hotel room's flickering neon light. The ceiling fan was buzzing as it turned above our heads. Then I looked at her curved eyelashes shaped like long, slim waves. She turned and looked at me with those eyes. My heart stopped. I saw her gorgeous brunette hair flowing down her neck. And then I saw her flawless naked back while she slipped out of her stockings. Finally, she turned and faced me, proudly burying my face into her breasts.

The contentment of being smothered with her love was written all over my face. No matter how hard I tried, I couldn't conceal the pleasure I felt. I just let it happen. Even as my mind was exploding with arousal, I forced my eyes open. There were now other passengers riding in our car. I was breathless. My forehead was covered in sweat. No one seemed to notice it except a couple of women seated across the aisle, glancing at me. They were witnessing a man madly in love and I sensed their approval. For a few moments, they offered their companionship on this solitary train ride and I was grateful.

When we arrived at Penn Station, my fellow women passengers got off and hurried along the platform where their companions were waiting for them, men from all corners of life. The women were hugged and kissed and held tightly, laughing with their mates. I asked myself, "Had I missed something in my previous life?" I never knew that there was so much love in this city. One has to be in love to see all the love that is around us.

38

THAT SAME EVENING, while I was still dreaming about Louisa, the telephone rang while I was in the shower at my place in the Riverdale section of the Bronx. At first I tried to ignore it because the hot water was rejuvenating my tired body and mind. But whoever was calling was persistent. The ringing stopped before I could get to the phone. And then it started ringing again when I got back under the shower head. On the third maddening attempt, I trod along the parquet floor with a towel wrapped around my waist. This time I reached the phone in time.

"Hello," I said with exasperation.

"Hello, Luke?"

"Marina? Is that you? What a nice surprise."

"I didn't think I was going to find you. I'm so happy you finally picked up the phone."

I heard her crying, but trying to suppress her tears.

"Marina, is everything okay?

"No, Luke, it's not okay at all!"

"What's going on over there? What's the problem?"

"They'll cut me off any minute now. But I don't care. I don't care! Do you hear me? I want everyone to hear me! Including you bastards who are listening in on this conversation right now! I'm not afraid of any of you!"

She couldn't hold back the tears any longer.

"Luke, are you still there?"

"Marina, please tell me what's going on?"

"They arrested Vasya! But when I went to the KGB building in Lubyanka, they told me that I should go to the local militia headquarters and file a missing person's report."

"Why would they arrest him? Last time he spoke to me, he said he didn't want to be involved with politics anymore. He said he only wants to spend time with you, Andrey and Grandma."

"It's the list, Luke."

"What list?"

"The list that your friends got published in the *Washington Post*. The list of dissidents."

"What? I don't understand."

"While interrogating you, the KGB agents replaced the list that Vasya gave to you with their own fake list. You know, the one that you were hiding in your boot? They put fake names on that list. So what the American newspaper published was a list of non-existent people, not dissidents. That gave them carte blanche to go after the real dissidents. And Vasya was high up on the KGB's internal list. He knows about all of it, he knows the Party's dirty secrets. And the KGB's, too. Luke, I'm afraid I'm never going to see my Vasya again!"

"Marina, calm down, please."

"You don't understand, it's total chaos over here, Luke. Everyone's celebrating."

"Wait, what are they celebrating?"

"My God, don't you see what's going on? Haven't you watched it happening on TV?"

"What's happening?"

"The Berlin Wall! They're tearing it down!"

"Really?"

"Yes! So now what's going to happen to us over here? Russia is no Germany! They arrested Vasya on November 8th, the day before the Wall came down. The KGB had it all planned out! Luke, can you please…?"

Without warning, the connection went dead. I was dumbfounded as terrifying thoughts raced through my mind. A fake list? The KGB getting Vasya? And what about all the other dissidents? Were they being rounded up too?

I turned the TV on in a hurry. There it was on every channel, that astonishing footage of thousands of people dismantling the Berlin Wall one gray cement block after another. The American newscaster was describing how the East Berlin television station had been overtaken by protesters and how the local intelligentsia were urging calm and national unity on the local radio.

While I was falling in love with Louisa, the old world order was collapsing along with the Berlin Wall in broad daylight for everyone to see. That was the date that would live in world history for everyone to remember: November 9th, 1989. The world changed that day because dissidents like Vasya and Lev had the courage to take that one first step.

Vasily, Vasya, my friend, where are you now? What happened to you? What were they doing to you? Finally, the Berlin Wall had come down, and with it, the end of the Cold War. But what about you and Lev and Anatoly and the others? This was supposed to be a day for you to celebrate. But instead, you were under arrest? This just didn't make sense. So had anything really changed? I guess this meant that the Bolsheviks and the KGB were still in charge.

My dark thoughts alarmed me. I had to go beyond my own dread and do something to help Vasya and the others. Wasn't that my mission after all? I needed to find Nicholas right away to see what could be done.

39

AS DAWN CAME, the rising sun colored the marshlands around my parked car with an otherworldly reddish glow. I had found some old towels in the trunk and used them for blankets so that I could curl up on the back seat and get a few hours of sleep. A cold damp sea breeze swept across the rest area where my car remained paralyzed. The breeze somehow penetrated inside, forcing me to wake up. I pulled a towel over my head for warmth, still not willing to budge. I was slowly waking up when I heard the heavy diesel pounding of a truck engine approaching. Powerful brakes on the truck brought the big semi and its rig to a screeching halt not far from my car. My eyes were wide open now. I sat up, still bleary-eyed, trying to re-focus.

I heard the truck's cabin door slam shut, and then the heavy footsteps of the driver walking behind my car, inspecting it from several angles. The guy came around and looked through my front window, knocking on the glass.

"Need some help, brother?" he asked in a strong, assertive voice.

The trucker was wearing a baseball cap and sported a couple day's growth of dark beard. He had on a white T-shirt that announced "THE LORD IS HERE" across his chest.

I squinted from the first rays of daylight.

"Help? What kind of help?" I said.

"You've gotta be quick, bro. Wake up! I have 5 tons of fragile merchandise in my truck that has to be delivered by 8am, today. And I still have many miles to cover. But we always help drivers in need."

"Thanks, but my problems are more than mechanical."

"Hey, I can't straighten out everything, bro, but what's the matter with you? Are you homeless? You hurt yourself?"

"Maybe all of that. But my car is the most pressing thing. It died and refuses to start up. Of course, I've been driving it pretty hard. I drove it all the way up here along the East Coast from Florida for a woman, a special woman."

"Hey, that's a long haul, I know. Done it myself. All for a woman? Now we have things in common. Pop the hood and let me look at your engine."

I pulled the lever inside my car and the hood snapped up, then the trucker opened it the rest of the way. He started his inspection, tugging wires, checking pumps, looking at the oil, and finally stepped back into view and held up something for me to see that I couldn't identify.

"Your starter cap was dirty," he announced matter-of-factly. He took out a big knife from a leather pouch on his belt and started cleaning the part. In less than two minutes, he had replaced the gizmo and called out:

"Try to start it now!"

I did as instructed. After a couple of tries, the engine kicked over and idled beautifully.

"Your starter wasn't just dirty, bro, it's worn out," he explained as he put his big hands on his knees and leaned his large frame down so he could look at me level-eyed through the window. "When you get to a city, you gotta change it out."

I looked at the truck driver in wonderment at his unpretentious expertise.

"You are eventually going to some city, right? After you see your 'special woman'? There's nothing out here."

"I think God sent you to me," I said, finally able to express my relief and appreciation.

"Amen," the driver said whole-heartedly. "Jesus Christ is our Lord and Savior. You a believer?"

"Not really. Well, maybe metaphorically, especially right now, but not literally."

"So if I fix your car 'metaphorically' will it run? I doubt it. And your starter cap is 'literally' garbage."

"Well, it depends in what philosophical category we are…"

"My name is Kirk by the way," he said matter-of-factly, managing a little smile.

"I'm Luke."

"Nice to meet you, brother. God is real. It ain't just some story. He's right here and He brought me to you. Come over to my truck, I've got some Bibles in my cab. I'm gonna give you one. That is, if you want it. No pressure."

"To be honest with you, Kirk," I began, "to be very honest with you …" But I couldn't think of how to finish my thought diplomatically, so I silently followed Kirk over to his big truck.

"Okay," I finally said. "What the hell. Give me one of your Bibles. You're very generous, thanks for all your help. I think you're a great guy."

"I'm giving you a leather edition," explained Kirk. "My pastor gave it to me. I think you need it more than I do."

We stopped by the big steps up to the driver's door on his semi. Suddenly, Kirk started breathing heavily. He sat down painfully on one of the steps and started rubbing the left side of his chest.

"Hey, Kirk. Are you okay?" I said.

"Oh, I'm fine. It's guilt, the guilt in my heart. It'll go away in a minute."

"What have you got to be guilty about?"

"When I was driving away from my wife and children at home, I looked at them in the rearview mirror and I could see the love in their eyes. I don't deserve them, man. See, I used to drink my worries away, popping pills that kept me awake, all that stuff. This line of work is hazardous, bro. It pays pretty well, but the shit you see on the road. Oh man, I don't want to even go there."

He took a deep breath and continued:

"Anyway, I'm good now. I turned things around, Luke. I go to my AA meetings, me and my wife, we are good. Except now I have this heart disease happening. But it'll go away, I have faith, see."

Kirk tapped on his heart with his big right hand.

"I have too much love in here for our Lord, bro. It won't stop. I was saved, so I know God is real. You gotta read the Good Book, Luke. All the answers are in there."

"Okay, I'll do it. You are a very good human being. I really appreciate you helping me out."

"Not really, I'm just following His instructions."

Kirk was taking deep breaths, like he was trying to regulate his heartbeat. I watched him with a worried look.

"Listen," I said gently, "you shouldn't be driving with chest pain."

"Gotta put food on the table, you know, a wife and two kids. God, I love them so much. What about you, Luke?"

"Wife and a kid. Margaret and Julian are their names."

Kirk pulled a bottle of pills out of his pocket and put a tablet under his tongue. He seemed to get some kind of instant relief from it.

"Hey, bro, those are pretty names, Margaret and Julian. God bless them and God bless you. I can tell you're a decent guy. It's their good fortune to have you in their lives, right?"

"Yes, I hope so. Thank you again. I appreciate everything you've done and everything you've said."

"Sure," said Kirk.

All of a sudden tears started rolling down Kirk's cheeks. Startled, I stared at him speechlessly. His tears had come out of nowhere. I was baffled by the intensity of his silent cry and at the same time I was at a loss on what to do and how to help. I sat down next to him for comfort.

"I'm sorry, Luke," said Kirk. "When these tears come, I can't stop them. The truth is I don't want to stop them. This must make you feel uncomfortable, seeing a grown-up man bawling like a baby. But my heart is aching and there ain't no medication out there that can cure the pain. I said I loved my wife and my children, but it's not the whole story. My story is much darker, deeper, and full of unexpected twists and turns. And it don't have a happy ending. Do you still want to hear it?"

"Yes, of course," I said hesitantly.

"So, my dear Luke, prior to taking off for the long haul, I've always felt that the road called out to me. I said my goodbyes to my wife, Agape and the kids. You know, my two boys, Zak and Wyatt. Supposedly she was going to drop them off at school afterwards. I drove off with a heavy heart, already missing them. You see, the first 100 miles of the road is always the hardest for me because I still feel I'm closer to home than to my destination. As I was reaching the 100 mile count that day, I remembered that I had left all my paperwork for the cargo on the bed stand.

"I was carrying very precious cargo that day. Toys. All toys, can you imagine? I thought I was having a joy ride, carrying that many smiles in the back of my truck. I made a U-turn. It took me two hours to make it back home and then..." Kirk's voice began trembling."...and then the worst thing happened, the worst event of my entire life when I walked back into my house."

Kirk took a deep breath as if diving into dangerous waters.

"At first, I saw his shoes," he continued." Then his coat in the living room. Then I heard them. She was moaning so loud. I never heard her making those sounds with me. I slowly opened the bedroom door. She had her legs spread wide open and Brian was on top of her, inside her, violating the sanctity of my home."

He turned and studied my face.

"Do you know what that means? Can you imagine that god-awful picture. I can't get it out of my head. I don't want to think about it anymore, but I'm unable to erase that image from my mind. Brian! My supposedly best friend and godfather to my children. That fucking little insurance agent, the Judas Iscariot who I had helped find work, who I gave our spare room to so he had a roof over his head. I even helped his sick mother move into an old-age home. And there was Brian fucking my wife in my own house. I wanted to shoot the fucker, but I didn't. 'Thy shall not kill' kept echoing in my brain, but my heart wanted me to pull the trigger and kill them both, you know?"

Kirk took a deep breath.

"But the worst part was that, after the surprise and the shock, when they were dressed and we sat down to talk about it in the kitchen, I began having palpitations. I couldn't breathe and I felt like my heart was being stabbed with hundreds of daggers. That's when I saw the evil in their eyes. They said they wanted to help me, but intentionally did it in slow motion, taking their time to bring me my medication, looking at one another suspiciously like conspirators.

"My wife's voice was cold, even though she was supposed to be feeling so sorry, so guilty. I understood right then what was going on. They both wished for me to be dead. Yes, I knew it deep down. My wife, the center of my life, who I loved so much, wished to see me dead!

"See, if I was dead now, nobody would've found out about their sordid affair. They would've gotten away with it. They'd get my house, my $200,000 life insurance money and my kids too. But God had a different plan. He, the Almighty, wanted me to live on. Why? Luke, do you know why? Why He wanted me to carry on? That's what I can't figure out. I called my pastor, I asked him to come by. Maybe he'd have an answer."

"It must have been very upsetting." I said. "You're a good man. You deserve so much better."

"I deserve no more happiness than you, or my wife, or even Brian. We all are God's children, Luke."

"I assume the common sense answer in this case, I mean in spe-cifically your case, would be forgiveness," I said. "But I don't know how to get there."

"You're very kind. I know my family is going to tell me to throw her out of my life. They all hate her. I mean she was a bitch to them for so long. She cut me off from everybody. But I loved her and I had the kids with her. I love my kids so much."

He paused and looked me directly into my eyes.

"Do you still have my Bible?"

"Yes, but I better give it back to you, Kirk. You need it more now than me."

"Thank you, Luke."

I handed Kirk's leather edition Bible back to him.

"I'm better now. Thanks for listening, Luke. Gotta get going. Don't forget to change that starter cap asap."

"Travel safe, Kirk. Thank you and God bless you."

"He already did. I met you!"

"Amen!" I said as he turned to get up into his truck. "Hallelujah!"

Kirk's big semi carefully maneuvered back on the road, accelerated and sped away. I found myself standing there, finally waving goodbye to him. He must have been looking at me in his rear-view mirror. He honked a few times as if re-affirming our singular encounter and the brotherly love that two strangers had exchanged on that solitary road.

I GOT BACK into my car and drove off on Langford Highway getting ever closer to my long-awaited rendezvous with Louisa. No sooner than I got up to speed, the rain came again and spread its fine, crystalline drops across my windshield. Within twenty minutes, it was pouring down hard, with the wind picking up, firing raindrops at me almost horizontally.

The rain was incessant, no matter the new state. The whole East Coast seemed to be under the deluge. Crossing from one state to another somehow affected my state of mind. Past and present were jumbled up until my cell phone rang, jerking me into the present. I checked the display and saw that it was Margaret. I let it go to message.

"Love, it's me. Just wondering how you are, and where you are. Julian's going to sing one of the leads at the school concert. He's so excited. Love, I miss you and I'm worried about you. Please don't forget your liver supplements. You always forget to take them. Where are you eating on your big drive? Where are you sleeping? I'm trying to picture you in my head all day long. I feel as if I'm on the road with you. Just wanted to tell you how much I miss you. Got to go now. Call me."

Throughout Margaret's message, I could hear the torment behind her stoic voice. I felt like banging my head on the steering wheel again for not picking up and having a normal conversation with her. Why couldn't I answer the call from my beloved wife and have a normal conversation?

Oh God, I didn't deserve a wife like her! Didn't Margaret really know I was going to see Louisa? Of course, she did! Why in Heaven's name did Margaret love me so much? Did one ever know why one loved another? Or how to measure it?

I knew this and I was recording these words very clearly. "I love my wife and I love Louisa. Damn it, I love them both! Oh, God, how am I going to get out of this in one piece?"

I wondered if my wife were really a saint? Maybe I'd make the call to God Himself and find out? Maybe Kirk was right. What if God was real? Would He even pick up the line on the other side? Would He patiently listen to me explaining the situation? Would He condone my leaving my wife and child, supposedly to drive a long way to interview for a job I had no intention of accepting? No way, I wasn't ever going to be a human rights lawyer again.

Not after what had happened.

Why was I lying to my wife Margaret and to my son Julian? Margaret knew. I could see it in her eyes when I left the house that morning. She knew where I was really going. She pretended to believe my phony story about the job opening and courageously hid her complete understanding of the truth. She was very good at playing the supportive wife. Damn good. The only hint of her inner dilemma was the slight trembling I noticed in her hands and the almost imperceptible tightening of her lips. My son was too young to notice any of the tension. Thank God for that.

Now I understood that Margaret was taking the gamble, betting all her chips on our marriage surviving this escapade. It was red or black, all in. I was either coming back to her, having resolved my love story with Louisa, closing that chapter of my life for once and for all. Or I was going away with 'the other woman' for good.

Not coming back? What about my son? What was I thinking? Margaret was so brave. I loved her and I knew she loved me. When she took me in her arms to kiss me goodbye before I got into the car, I felt her heart beat so powerfully that it seemed ready to explode inside her chest. I caressed her cheeks where a cascade of tears were dammed up, waiting to gush out but didn't. When she looked into my eyes, I briefly saw her fear. But as always, she kept her inner turmoil to herself. She put on a brave smile and wished me a safe trip. Her kiss was long and passionate. She couldn't stand to see me drive off.

So why did she let me go?

My wife liked things clear, crystal clear, with no complications. She herself was as lucid and transparent as spring water. Where did she find the strength and the courage to let me go so I could make sense of my heart and mind?

I didn't even want to think about the "but what if"? It wasn't fair what I was doing to Margaret. How had she tolerated me all these years already? I'd been a drunk. I'd lied. I'd been half-present most of the time. I'd gotten angry. I'd been aggressive, picking fights with strangers indiscriminately. I'd been impatient, self-destructive and confused.

But I did love her. In my own strange way, I did. And I still loved her. It's just different now. I can't explain it. Just different.

I pulled my car over to the side of road and cut the engine. The rain had stopped and a thick fog was drifting in off the ocean, making the road impossible to see. It looked exactly like the brain fog in my head. Finally I had to admit to myself that I was exhausted from the persistent bad weather that was tormenting this journey, from outside and even more from inside.

"Margaret, Margaret," I repeated my wife's name.

Somehow, if she were next to me, it would feel safer, no matter the weather conditions.

"Hey, Margaret, can you come here, please."

Now I was yelling at the top of my lungs.

"Margaret, do you hear me? Don't leave me alone here, please? I miss you!"

I closed my eyes and let the wind do the crying. When I opened my eyes again, I was starting my 41st circle around the sun and this time I was not coming back to the same place. That was a promise.

I EMBARKED UPON this crazy odyssey for a supposed job interview in New York. That ploy wouldn't even have come together if Margaret hadn't thrown a surprise birthday party for me at our place in Key West. I'm about 1,500 miles away from there right now, and only a couple months had passed since the birthday party. Yet that peculiar event seemed to have happened in a different galaxy, in a different lifetime.

That day in the Florida Keys was like every other day, sunny and cloudless. Late that afternoon, I drove home from the Monroe County Courthouse, also known as Freeman Justice Center on Fleming Street, where I worked as a public defender for a flock of penniless felons. Our quaint, palm-lined street was eerily still. Not a soul was anywhere in sight. No one was mowing their lawns nor washing their SUVs. The reality of my everyday life was drearily predictable. I pulled into our driveway and parked behind Margaret's car. It was just the end of another dreadful day.

When I opened the front door, I was stunned to find our place packed with people shouting my name, cameras flashing and corks popping out of champagne bottles.

"Happy Birthday, Luke! Happy Birthday!" they screamed in unison.

Oh, God, how I wanted to ignore my 40th just like I had tried to ignore all my birthdays. But Margaret obviously thought that it was a milestone that had to be celebrated.

So there I was, standing in shock at the front door, staring at all the people in our home, speechless, exhausted, unshaven, and suddenly covered in cold sweat. I moved my glazed eyes through the crowd in disbelief, trying to find one welcome face until I spotted Nicholas.

"You came all the way from D.C. for this crap?" I shouted at him.

He pointed at Margaret, hinting as if he had no choice. Suddenly she was in front of me with her arms around my neck, whispering into my ear:

"Many happy returns of the day, my love."

Before I could respond, she landed a kiss on my lips that turned into a long, flaming smack in full display for all our guests to admire. Surprised, I kissed her back so as not to disappoint the spectators. And she responded with an even more fiery, intense kiss. It went on and on, unending. The partygoers started exchanging embarrassed looks, but Margaret didn't seem to care. She kept on kissing me. Finally, she pulled her lips away after what seemed an eternity to me. The crowd had gotten quiet, so when she turned back to face everyone, they all had a slightly baffled look on their faces.

The situation seemed terribly comical to Margaret and she burst into uncontrollable laughter. I had never seen her laugh harder, giggling, then howling and finally cackling, her laughter ringing out unabashedly. It was so contagious that, one by one, all our guests joined in. Now everybody was laughing.

The silliness of the scene was impossible to resist, so I too joined in, though the look on my face must have been one of bewilderment, not merriment. As she caught her breath, Margaret put her arms around me and hugged me one more time.

"Happy 40th, my dear Luke," she whispered into my ear. "My wish is for you to love me as much as I love you."

Without giving me a chance to answer her with any of my half-truths, Margaret took my hand and led me into the living room where I was surrounded by well-wishers. I shook all the hands and kissed all the cheeks I could, then extricated myself, going through our kitchen, grabbing a cold beer from the frig, and slipping outside to the patio for a little peace.

There, I found Nicholas behind our gas-powered, stainless steel barbecue, grilling burgers and hot dogs for the hungry hordes of party-goers. He was wearing a chef apron and seemed to be enjoying his Kitchen Patrol duty. I was so relieved to find someone I could talk to.

"Bless you, my friend," I said, "for being here."

"Wouldn't have missed it for anything," said Nicholas.

I was also relieved to find my son, Julian, who gave me his perfunctory "Hi, Dad," while focusing on all the sizzling paddies on the grill. My boy had already slathered up a bun with thick goops of mustard and ketchup, impatiently awaiting the sizzling burger that Nicholas now flipped onto Julian's paper plate.

"Are you coming back?" asked Nicholas.

"No way, José."

"Luke, be serious. You can't be a public defender for the rest of your life. More than ever, we need you in human rights."

"Younger lawyers are out there, ready to jump in."

"You are one of the brightest and bravest people working in our field."

"Listen, Nick, that's not the guy I see every morning in the mirror."

"Still, they want you back. There's an opening with an important New York firm. You'd be perfect for them. They're working on Sudan. Didn't you see on CNN what's happening over there? It's horrible, almost two million people are trapped in a famine zone with no help in sight. They're mostly women and children of course. The world has gone mad, my friend. We've got to do something about it."

I listened respectfully to my friend's plea, then I told him: "Nick, this world has always been mad, nothing has changed. Except now we have CNN to tell us about it. I can't do it anymore. We've talked about this before."

I fixed him with my eyes so he could see my resolve.

"I just can't. I'm done."

I spotted Margaret in the backyard with a group of guests, chatting happily, laughing, looking every bit the unruffled hostess. The people gathered around her seemed to relish every word she said, every gesture she made.

"She's a gem," said Nick, glancing at Margaret as well. "You're so lucky to have her."

"An award should be given to my wife for…"

Nicholas looked at me with a question mark on his face until I finished the thought:

"…for putting up with me."

I took another gulp of cold beer, turned back to Nicholas and purposefully changed my frivolous tone.

"What's the name of that firm?"

"Rosenbach, Garfield, Marsh & Browman."

"What harm could come from just meeting them?"

"That's the spirit!" said Nicholas with genuine enthusiasm. "I'll set it up for you."

"You're a great man, my friend."

"No," said Nicholas, "It's you who's made a real difference, not me. One of the partners, Brian Rosenbach, told me they can get some Hollywood celebrities for you."

"Celebrities?" I laughed. "Those starving people need protection and food, not some fucking Hollywood types. Don't you see what's wrong with that picture?"

"You're right, Luke, just go with your instinct."

"I'm not going anywhere. But if I ever do, this time you're coming with me."

"It's a deal!"

My buddy, Nicholas, was ready to say anything just to get me back into the human rights game. Even if I could smell bullshit a mile away, his sincere esteem was still welcome.

The rest of the party was a blur, probably because I drank several more beers to numb the boredom of it all. I do remember me hugging Nicholas and thanking him for coming. After he left for the airport, I also recall the tropical rainstorm that thankfully blew in from the Gulf of Mexico and chased off the last stubborn guests.

Our home was a gigantic mess, but finally it was quiet enough to hear a human voice that wasn't yelling some empty compliment or polite nonsense at me. Margaret and I were sitting on the sofa in the living room, enjoying the calm after the storm. Julian had conked out in his room from an overdose of barbecue, soft drinks and birthday cake. Balloons, empty bottles and dirty paper plates with uneaten food were all over the place. Margaret was drinking a final glass of champagne from a plastic flute, observing me closely as she sipped the bubbly.

"Nicholas wants me to interview with a New York firm."

"I thought you were finished with human rights work?"

"I am. But it doesn't hurt to talk with them."

"No, it doesn't hurt," she says, taking my hand with hers. "Maybe it's time we talked, too."

"About what?"

"Do you …? Do you love me?" asked Margaret ever so softly.

"I do love you, Margaret."

"I needed to hear that."

I sensed Margaret was a little relieved, though her voice was still trembling.

"Honey," I said to her, "You made a wonderful party."

"And you hated almost every moment of it."

I declined to respond. I stood up and started putting trash into a big black plastic garbage bag. After a minute of silence, I turned back toward her.

"If they're interested in me, I'm going up to New York for the interview. It may turn out to be something."

My words almost drove my wife to tears, but she held them back bravely. Margaret understood immediately that the interview was a ruse for me to go off on my own. But she said nothing, just nodding her head in silent accord. Staring at me plaintively, her sad eyes begged me to stop thinking about the other woman. I stared back at her. My eyes said I couldn't.

"DAY IN THE country," was the cryptic message Louisa left me, along with the exact spot to meet her: the northeast corner of 27th Street and the West Side Highway.

That was ten years ago, but I still remember every detail as if it were yesterday. I reached our rendezvous spot ahead of schedule so as not to make her wait.

Right on time, she pulled up in her white Corvette and stopped on a dime next to me. I leaned down with a big smile on my face. Neither of us said a word. Words were not necessary. Then I walked around to her side of the car and opened her door, motioning with my hands that it was my turn to drive. She laughed with that delightful laugh of hers and slid her luscious body over to the passenger seat without a whimper.

I pulled out and accelerated to keep pace with the massive crush of trucks and cars heading out of the city next to the Hudson River. People were driving home to the suburbs after another day of work. We said nothing to each other, but she put her right hand on my thigh and turned to study me closely. I kept my eyes on the road, but I couldn't help seeing peripherally how she was staring so intently at me.

"What?" I said finally.

She didn't respond, still keeping her eyes steady on my face, though with a playful look of sudden discovery.

"What?" I asked again. "Why are you looking at me like that?"

Without a word, she climbed on top of my lap, throwing her legs over my shoulders and started kissing me. I was trying to steer the car in the traffic, leaning my head one way and the other to see the highway around her hair. All the while cars were zipping by us. She covered my face with passionate kisses.

"Hey, what are you doing?" I said, panicking a little.

She didn't seem to hear me nor had she any intention of stopping the kisses. I was about to plow into the car in front of us which had to slow down suddenly, so I stamped on the Corvette's brakes. We stopped abruptly and I heard other cars screeching to a halt behind us. Horns were honking angrily at me and a massive line of vehicles of all sizes was backed up behind Louisa's Corvette. Drivers of cars in either lane were passing us on the right and left, shouting furious insults at us as they moved by. Louisa hardly noticed all the mayhem. She just kept kissing me with a force and focus that was mind-boggling. Traffic jam? She just didn't care a whit about traffic jams.

As much as I wanted to try to advance the car, I couldn't resist the taste of her lips. I started kissing her back, now blind to all the traffic, engulfed in her fire. The Corvette came to a complete halt. As cars and trucks made their way around us and traffic on the West Side Highway started to flow again, our paralysis in the middle lane of the busy thoroughfare became even more dangerous. Any moment now, we might be slammed. But miraculously, passing cars and trucks slowed down and seemed to detour around us carefully, as if they didn't want to disturb us. Drivers were lowering their windows and gazing at us in awe, trying to catch a glimpse of our daring circus act.

We became the West Side Highway's suicidal love attraction. After they got a glimpse of us kissing deeply, drivers sped away and new ones appeared. Each face was different. They were like balloons floating by in the corners of our eyes, some raging mad, some envious, some giving us the finger or the peace sign, others crossing their wrists as if they wished someone would arrest us.

All of a sudden it occurred to me that it wasn't us who were the attraction. It was the world that was on stage. The world of people passing by our parked car was the real theater, Louisa and I, the audience. All these faces were a carousel of unique characters wearing masks and costumes from their own plays. Our love provoked them.

It insulted them, it inspired them, it embraced them, it amused them, and, for a precious few, it brought tears to their eyes.

Both of us realized that parked there in the middle of that highway circus, we might die in each other's arms, crushed by a 16-ton tanker. But it simply didn't matter. Danger, pain, punishment, nothing mattered anymore. Our love was bigger than any highway, bigger than any bridge or city or country, bigger than the world. We had created a universe where nothing could stop us from loving one another.

We kept on kissing and cars kept going around us, respecting our island of love. She unbuttoned my shirt, her hands so tender. She touched my neck and chest and I felt her palms sweating just like before. She was breathless as I slid my hands between her thighs, her body convulsed, silently screaming that she was ready for me. In the depths of her eyes, I saw the untamed gazelle running wild again and there was no turning back.

Afterwards, I put the idling Corvette into gear and sped away, passing under the George Washington Bridge and upstate along the Taconic. We were silent for the entire drive, physically silent. Our mouths were not moving, nor did we utter any sounds whatsoever. But what was happening in the car between us was the opposite of silence. It was a symphony of devotion exploding inside our souls, expanding our universe. The rain had stopped so we opened the windows. Cool winds blew in, caressing and playing with her hair, then ricocheting off me, leaving all her scents on my skin and in my nostrils. I could smell all her thoughts of love, all her desires, all her hopes. Buried underneath her beauty, I was feeling alive. Like a newborn, I was tasting life like I'd never known it existed. All just by sitting next to her.

LOUISA TOLD ME to exit the highway at the sign that said Bear Mountain State Park. Once we were moving toward the park gate, she had me turn off the paved road onto a gravel one used only by park rangers. We curved up and around into the heart of the forest. The gravel soon disappeared. Now the road was nothing more than a narrow, pockmarked dirt pathway snaking up the verdant hillside through poplars, maples and pine trees. Her Corvette was not made for trail-blazing, so before I cracked an axle, I stopped the car and turned off the engine. We got out, clasped hands and walked up the pathway through the woods to a delightful plateau covered with countless willow trees, all standing side by side like old friends, their narrow leaves and slender twigs swaying gently in the afternoon breeze.

We walked into the willows without exchanging a word, delighting in the sounds and smells and speckled sunlight. Then without warning, she let go of my hand and ran off. I followed her as best I could, pushing aside the leafy branches, but lost sight of her. I followed her laughter, first across a creek with gurgling water, then through thicker woods. Her laughter echoed throughout the forest, making it difficult for me to figure out where it was coming from. Birds at the tops of the trees joined in, chanting, cawing, warbling along with her. I wasn't sure if I was getting closer to her, but no matter, I had to pause to catch my breath. The afternoon sun shot violet and orange shafts of light across the mountains, striking the undulating tops of all the trees with glittering luminosity.

I heard her calling my name. Or was it just the wind rustling the leaves? I started running after her again, past century-old trees who seemed totally unimpressed by the mad lovers racing under their boughs. It was their forest, not ours. We were intruding on their home. Hadn't they already seen it all? The wildest loves? The most enraptured couplings? They would bend a little in deference to our energy, but it was more likely a sign of their disdain. They were probably wondering what the hell were these fragile, misguided creatures doing in their land of deep roots, gnarly branches and massive trunks?

It was all magnificently new to me. As I ran, I breathed in the forest's pungent, moist air. I was guided only by Louisa's enchanting scent somewhere up ahead. The treetops were so crowded that only a little sunlight penetrated down to the forest's floor. I came out in a grassy, open area surrounded by mimosas and ash trees in silent vigil.

The silence in this meadow was profound, as if all sound had been sucked out of the earth. I stood completely still, listening for a clue to her whereabouts. The quiet was interrupted by the singsong of a far-off sparrow. Then I heard light footsteps approaching me from behind and I felt her hands touching my shoulders, like a gentle breeze. She put her arms under mine and squeezed me from behind.

I turned around to her and discovered she had already taken off all her clothes, except for her sneakers. She helped me get undressed and then led me over to a nest she had already scouted out in the center of the meadow. Together we sank onto a thick, grassy bed and were covered by a blanket of wild flower fragrances. The sun was moving lower in the western skies and the forest was bathed in a hazy, cotton-soft light.

I covered her entire body with untamed kisses. My lips were trembling as I tasted her sweet juices. She was serene even as her breathing accelerated. She welcomed me inside her and raised her hips to greet me, scissor-gripping her legs around my waist to bring our bodies together even more powerfully.

I was so deep inside her I felt as if I was making love to the meadow and the forest and the flowers and the trees. To the Earth itself! The moment was so grand I felt we were sharing it with hundreds of other couples, all making love in meadows all over the world. They were all out there and I alone could hear the far-off symphony of their cries of pleasure. God, thank you for this perfect orgy! I was in love with the world, a world that was loving me back through this passionate woman. Louisa and I were one. That made me one with the world.

I opened my eyes and discovered teardrops rolling down her cheeks. I was confused until she smiled at me, showing me that they were tears of joy. To my surprise, my eyes were awash with tears too. I didn't know where they had come from because I never cry, never. They were salty tears. Maybe it was the sea inside me overflowing with waves of happiness.

I rolled off of her and we lied hand-in-hand with our heads touching, staring at the pink clouds sailing above us in the dusk sky. Watching that cosmic spectacle, I felt we were the tiniest creatures in the world? Louisa and I were nothing but minuscule, meaningless beings, yet somehow as sacred as children.

In my innocence, I was blessed with the joy of prayer. I saw clearly I had remained a child all my life. Like a child, I opened my arms and I welcomed the world. Like a child, I wanted to scream with joy. Like a child, all I wanted to do was play.

I wasn't afraid anymore, not afraid of being myself. For once in my life, for one brief moment in cosmic time, I was perfect. I screamed with joy as loud as I could. Flocks of birds resting in the trees all over the forest were disturbed. I could tell by all the chirping and squawking that they were commenting on my outburst. Maybe they didn't understand me, so I screamed again. Louisa giggled at all the birdcalls coming from the forest. She understood and finally all the birds did too. They understood that an overjoyed child was celebrating his homecoming. They understood how much I was in love with this woman next to me and they understood how much I was in love with the world. Finally, I was home.

We both closed our eyes, exhausted from so many intoxicating emotions and in perfect harmony with nature. I didn't know how long we slept in that grassy meadow. But when I next opened my eyes, the sky and trees had disappeared, blocked out by the fog that had rolled over the forest without a murmur. It almost seemed like we'd slept through spring and summer and woken up in the middle of autumn.

The temperature had dropped too. The fog was so thick I could barely see my hand in front of my face. A strange muffled silence had descended over the forest and nothing stirred.

Suddenly I heard gunshots and dogs barking in the distance. Then more gunshots, a little closer. I got up, understanding immediately that a group of hunters and their hounds were steadily moving towards us.

My stirring woke up Louisa. I leaned down and gently touched her face.

"Wake up, my love."

She blinked her eyes. More gunshots rang out.

"What's that?"

"We need to go. Get dressed."

"Okay. I hung my clothes on a tree over there."

She could hardly see the tree in the fog, but set off in the right direction.

"Found the tree," she called out.

I readjusted my eyes and started looking for where I left my shirt and trousers. They were nowhere to be found.

"I can't find my dress," Louisa called out.

"Oh shit," I whispered.

We kept looking in vain for our things.

"I can't believe someone stole our stuff!" she said. "All the way out here? Everything?"

I looked down at my shoes and her sneakers and silently thanked God we weren't barefoot.

"Why would they do that?" she said.

"I don't know," I said, rolling my eyeballs, recognizing that the situation was both funny and desperate.

"What are we going to do now?" she asked.

"Follow me," I said, "Let's go find your car."

NAKED LIKE ADAM and Eve, we started jogging back toward the car. A waxing moon had risen in the east, casting a cold, fuzzy illumination over the forest and lighting the way for us. Louisa went in front, with grass and flowers caught in her flowing hair, dirt and leaves stuck on her bouncing backside. Powerful and sexy, she had the aura of an Amazonian princess moving gracefully in the moonlight.

I tried to keep up with her swift pace, but every muscle in my body was strained to its limits. Born and bred in the wild, I was a caveman hunter with my woman, master of the forest and all its wildlife. Finally, we were free from the man-made world. We had been liberated from the constraints of civilization.

The fog had lifted a little and we made it back to the place in the gravel road where I had parked her Corvette. Except the car was no longer there. Fresh tire tracks on the road showed where some-body must have hot-wired the engine, turned the vehicle around and driven it away down the hillside.

"Car thieves! Out here?" Louisa said, enraged.

"Shhh," I whispered, hearing the hunters and their dogs getting closer. "We need to find a hiding place."

I grabbed Louisa's hand and guided her through the trees to the foot of a cliff that I had first noticed on the way up the hillside earlier in the day. We hurried along the rocks until I spotted a black hole in the stone face of the cliff. I led her inside.

The smell in the cave was strong, as if other wild animals had used it recently as a hideout. I pulled Louisa down close to me when I heard the hunters' party and their hounds getting closer. In the half shadows, we saw a family of wild boars scampering past our cave, Mama, Papa and several little boars, fleeing for their lives.

"So that's what they're hunting," I whispered.

I jumped up and grabbed her hand.

"Let's get down to the highway and hitch a ride."

She just stared at me with a frail look.

"I don't think I can go on," she said. "Not without some clothing. And I'm thirsty."

"I'm going to get you something to drink and something to wear. We passed a Park Ranger depot before."

"How will you find it again?"

"Easy. It was 9 trees on the left from the turn off, behind the pond, with the bird house on the 3rd fencepost."

"Ever been here before?"

"No, I noticed it earlier. I count things and store details away. A habit from childhood. Very useful on a foggy night."

I kissed the tips of her cold fingers.

"We need to move," I said. "Let's go."

We made it to the pond and scooped up chilly water in our cupped hands to drink gratefully. The Park Ranger depot was a run-down warehouse with a tin roof. We approached it cautiously. From behind a massive oak tree, I checked the place out. The property was fenced in with a horse stable and a chicken coop. There was no sign of anybody around and, most importantly, there weren't any dogs. I saw a bunch of faded horse blankets airing out on the fence.

After waiting a couple more minutes to make sure that the Park Rangers had gone home, I ran over to the fence and grabbed a couple of the blankets, then sprinted back to Louisa behind the oak tree. We wrapped the horse blankets around ourselves like towels in a sauna, delighted to feel some warmth and cover, though they stank of horse sweat. We stayed there until the sound of the hunters and dogs had faded away somewhere up the foggy hillside. Then we quickly re-traced our steps down the pathway and back to the gravel road, finally coming out on the shoulder of the highway.

We must have been quite a sight in our horse blankets because nobody would stop to pick us up, no matter how much I waved my arms for help. One couple driving by in a camper looked at us like extra-terrestrials. They slowed down, but refused to stop, their bulging eyes glued to us as they passed, making us feel like animals who had just escaped the zoo.

Finally, a farm truck loaded with crates of fruits and vegetables approached. It was creeping along in the fog with its bright lights on. I stepped out in the middle of the highway with my hands in the air, bare-chested, wearing only the horse blanket around my waist, beseeching the driver to stop. He braked hard and stopped his truck only a few feet in front of me.

"Jesus, are you mad, man?" the truck driver cried.

"Yes, I am," I said. "Thanks for stopping."

Louisa emerged from the bushes, the horse blanket wrapped under her arms with some cleavage showing. Looking at both of us, the farmer burst out laughing.

"What the hell! Are you guys lost? What's with the tribal costumes?"

"Can you give us a lift to the nearest town?" I asked.

"Sure, hop in," said the farmer. "Don't worry about a thing. I used to be a nudist too, but just got tired of the colony members."

The friendly farmer eased his clutch into gear on his truck and we moved forward, lumbering down the highway.

"My name's Joe."

"Nice to meet you, Joe. I'm Louisa, this is Luke."

"How did you two end up here?"

"The fog," I said. "We got lost in the fog. And then someone stole our car."

"Shit, man, I'm sorry for the locals. They hate people like you. They're so narrow-minded. They have a crazy preacher at the local church who stirs them up. He despises nudists. You aren't bothering anybody? Hey, Adam and Eve started out naked, right?

"Naked and free," I said.

"Yeah, naked and free," repeated Joe, with empathy.

"Listen, Joe," I explained. "We aren't really nudists."

"Who are you then?"

"Just a man and a woman in love."

"Are you guys out of your mind? Walking around here at night like that?"

"They stole our clothes too," said Louisa.

"Damn, sorry about that. See what I told you about the locals? You can get killed around here for taking off your clothes in the first place! They think it's a sin."

"We love danger," I said. "And we love sinning."

"I can see," said Joe. "I can definitely see that."

"Sorry to disappoint you," added Louisa.

"Oh, I'm not disappointed at all. Nudism is no big deal," said Joe, shaking his head. "Are you hungry? Everything in the back of the truck is fresh. I'm an organic farmer, the real deal. Help yourself!"

"Thanks, Joe," said Louisa. "You're a very nice ex-nudist."

"I like you too," said Joe. "If there were more people like you at the nudist colony, I might even rejoin. But then I'm already 'at one with nature,' like they say."

Before I could tell Joe how much we had been communing with nature that day, he pulled his truck over abruptly, put his gears into reverse and backed up a short distance. Then he pointed at something on the access road off to the side of the highway. Through the fog, we made out the outline of Louisa's Corvette.

"Your car, no?"

"I'm afraid so."

"You're lucky. They took it on a joy ride and dumped it close by," said Joe, grabbing a big flashlight. "Let's see if we can get it started."

While Louisa stayed in the truck, Joe and I checked out the damage. Somebody had stolen the car's stereo system, but otherwise, the Corvette was intact.

"They hotwired it," said Joe, flashing a beam of light through the window on the driver's side. Stripped wires from the broken ignition switch were hanging below the dashboard. I got in and jiggled the wires together. The engine turned over and came to life.

"Thanks for everything, Joe," said Louisa, with a handful of carrots and apples from the back of the truck.

"Glad to be of help," said Joe. "You two, take care."

We got back into the idling Corvette. I turned it around and headed back to the city. In his kindly way, Joe was waiting in his truck until we made a U-turn and passed in front of him. He waved goodbye to us as we sped away.

45

DESPITE THE FACT that a couple of gadgets on the dashboard were broken and the leather back seat was missing, I was able to drive Louisa's car back to my place in the Bronx. Thanks to the fog, it took twice as long as the drive up the Hudson Valley and thanks to our horse blankets, it smelled like a stable inside the Corvette. So we took them off and opened the windows. First on the highway and then afterwards, on the city streets, hardly anyone noticed our bare shoulders. I found a parking spot not far from my place in Riverdale, pulled in and gratefully stopped the car engine. As we prepared to once again put on the horse blankets and scramble from the car to the entrance of my apartment building, Louisa turned to me and put her hand on my arm.

"Want to know what was on my mind this morning?" she asked.

"Of course."

"I was wondering what the most important word in my life is."

"And?"

"'Freedom.' Being free is the most important thing for me. I felt free with you today."

"Let's feel free in a hot bath," I said with a kiss.

We opened the car doors and dashed for the building's entrance, laughing like crazy people, much to the amusement of other pedestrians on the sidewalk. As soon as we got inside my front door, we dropped the horse blankets on the parquet floor and I ran hot water in the bathtub. The blankets ended up in a plastic garbage bag and we ended up lounging in each other's arms in the bathtub.

The cuts, bruises and sore muscles from our adventures in the country yearned for the peace and tranquility of steaming hot water. I turned off all the electric lights and lit a solitary candle that flickered on the edge of the tub. We lounged together in the bubble bath, silently reflecting about what we had just experienced. We were no longer tribal savages making love on the grass and hiding in a cave from wild animals and hunters. Now we were typical New York urbanites, staring at the spider spinning his web in a corner of the high ceiling, ensnared ourselves in a concrete jungle of our own making.

Did today even happen or was it all a beautiful dream? I kissed Louisa deeply and tried to figure out where our love story was heading.

"I don't know anything about you," I whispered to her.

"What do you want to know?"

"Everything.

"I don't know everything about myself," she said with that laugh of hers. "It's a work-in-progress."

"Let's start with what you do."

"You mean professionally?"

I kissed her.

"I'm a writer," she said when our lips separated. "If you can call writing a profession."

"What kind of writing?"

"Poetry."

"A poet?"

"Yes. Surprised?"

She kissed me.

"I would have never guessed it," I said when our lips separated.

"I like putting my life into verse. Or verse into my life. What did you think I did?"

"Magician? The way you pull off your disappearing act?"

We both laughed and kissed again.

"It's because I was scared. I still am. I'm scared about what I'm feeling. That's the truth. And I'm glad I got it off of my chest. What about you?"

"I'm still recovering from the forest," I confessed.

"No kidding," she whispered. "With you, it was love at first sight. I never believed that that even existed. Maybe I didn't want to believe it."

I kissed her more.

"Once I was in a terrible relationship with an abusive, controlling man. He hurt me badly. He really did. When I finally dared to end our relationship, I said to myself that I was going to live my life to the fullest."

I wrapped my arms around her waist and, spoon-like, pulled her back against my chest.

"I was going to live out all my fantasies, no matter how outrageous they were, and that included even buying sex, if I felt like it."

"Every man dreams about being your whore, honeypie. Except I hope that that particular fantasy has been scratched off the list!"

"You don't have to worry, my love. I've done most of them with you. Only one is left."

"Well, now I'm scared."

"I want to make love on a boat in the middle of the ocean. Does that excite you?"

"I'm more prone to motels, hotels, cars, anything that's available at that moment. From here on, you can add forests to my list."

"Got it, you want the fastest route to the humpy-pumpy machine."

"Pretty much so. At least that's been my game until I met you."

"And?"

"And what?"

"Since you met me, what happened?"

I was silent. Words, where were you? My mind was like a car radio scanning the spectrum non-stop, skipping from one station to another, without ever making any sense. All I could hear was incomprehensible cosmic blather. I laughed nervously at my own mental paralysis. She laughed with me.

"I hear you," she said in total seriousness. "You don't have to find the right words. I know how you feel without you telling me."

It was at that precise moment when I knew. I knew Louisa was my "immortal beloved," the kind of lover that the great Beethoven dedicated all his music to, a love that even death cannot obstruct.

"What about you? What do you do?" she asked. "Let me guess. You go to a fucked-up clubs like The Hole and drink Holy Grail cocktails, the absolute shittiest martini in the history of all mixed beverages ever. Between you and me, only desperate people go to god-forsaken places like The Hole. Aren't they just looking to get smashed and get laid? And not in that order?

"You're describing most of the people I know, with very few exceptions."

"You must have been very lonely and very depressed. What kind of profession makes a wonderful guy like you feel that lonely and depressed? Stockbroker? No, you're not the type. Surgeon? No, you're too impetuous! War reporter? That's it! I've got it, you must be a journalist obsessed with sex and alcohol, living on the edge?"

"Sex happened only when you overpowered me. Before you, I was content with just getting smashed. It's you who overpowered my free will."

"You mean you fell in love."

"Lawyers' talk for 'I fell hard for you.'"

"You're a lawyer?"

"Do I hear disappointment in your voice?"

"What kind of lawyer?"

"I mostly deal with people whose rights have been unjustly violated."

"Human rights?"

"Exactly."

"Now I know why I fell so madly in love with you!" she said, kissing me passionately. "You're out there saving people's lives!"

"'Saving people's lives' is a bit too much. Protecting their rights is more accurate."

"Is that why your head was bandaged in DC? That was after one of your dangerous missions?"

"It didn't seem dangerous, at least at first. I was in Russia meeting dissidents, so that we could get their names published in the

States. Apparently, the Soviets won't touch known dissidents any more. I'm not sure that's the case any longer."

"I'm so blind. I assumed you hurt yourself coming home drunk from some bar."

"Why were you in the train station?"

"Nothing so dangerous. I was attending the annual Dead Poets Society meeting. It's named after the movie."

She stepped out of the bath and stood unblushingly in front of me in all the pink glory of the original Eve.

"You want to hear a poem?"

"Of course I do."

"Sun down.
Torn clouds.
Still no moon.
I am this night sky."

"Beautiful. When did you write that?

"That's not mine. Ishikawa Takoboku wrote it a hundred years ago. Do you mind if I smoke?"

"Not at all."

She lit a cigarette and sat down on the toilet seat.

"Do you like my body?"

"I'm crazy about it."

Louisa took a puff on the cigarette, pondering if she should reveal more of her feelings. I saw in her eyes that she decided to take the short cut.

"Anyway, that's how I was feeling before I met you."

"And now?"

"It was many and many a year ago,
In a kingdom by the sea
That a maiden there lived whom you may know
By the name of Annabel Lee,
And this maiden she lived with no other thought
Than to love and be loved by me."

She looked at me with tears rolling down her cheeks.

"That's Poe," she said. "But Unamuno gets me even better. *Piensa el sentimento, siente el sentimento.* I think the feeling and I feel the thought."

She took a puff on the cigarette and looked at me hard.

"You'll never ever leave me, right?"

"Only when I'm dead."

"Never say that," she said. "Never, ever say that!"

She stepped into the bath again and buried my head in between her full breasts, wrapping her arms around me.

"I'm so scared of losing you. Oh, God, please do not ever let us separate!"

She started sobbing quietly, covering my head with gentle kisses. I was enchanted yet puzzled by her sincere sense of tragedy and hope.

"God of Eternity," I pleaded to the cosmic void inside my head, "Please never let me forget the emotions in this bathroom tonight."

I no longer wanted to remember the past or dream about the future. All I wanted was for this moment to be frozen, multiplied and expanded. There was no oxygen left in the bathroom, only the love we were breathing in. As she pressed her wet lips to mine, my mind was frantically searching for a prayer.

"Pray," I heard the voice inside my head say back to me. "Pray that this love story with Louisa never ends because there can't be any life without your Immortal Beloved."

46

FOR SEVEN DAYS and seven nights, our bodies, minds and souls did not communicate with anything but each other, not needing anything in the outer world. I was her universe and she was mine. The apartment I lived in at the time – on Johnson Avenue within earshot of the Spuyten Duyvil station on the Metro-North line – became the center of our planetary system. We made love morning, noon and night, joining all our body parts in sensual and sometimes funny ways. Eyes, mouths, fingers, toes, hairs, lips, breasts, ears and noses. Everything became part of our lovemaking, be it eating, shaving, reading, napping or bathing. Even when we lay exhausted next to each other in total silence, we were astounded by the exhilaration that we felt in each other's peaceful presence. We were two love addicts who couldn't get enough of our own high.

The telephone was unplugged and only used to order sushi and Thai take-out that was delivered to my front door. The television was never turned on, and my mail was left to accumulate in the metal box down in the lobby.

The following Monday morning, I decided to plug my telephone back into its wall socket in the living room. Then I went to the window, looked outside and opened it for some fresh air. Immediately, the far-off urban cacophony outside seeped inside our nest, a blend of parents yelling at their children, a fire truck siren screeching in the distance and buses cruising by. From my living room window, I caught a glimpse of the Harlem River and the college skull crews out there on the water rowing upstream.

As quickly as I could, I closed the window tight because Louisa was still sleeping and I didn't want her to be disturbed. I plugged the TV in, but refused to turn it on so that we could be spared the horrendous news that most certainly awaited us. My phone started to ring. I picked up the receiver and instantly put it down again. Then I buried the entire telephone under a big pillow on the couch to muffle the next caller.

I glanced back at Louisa still asleep on my king-size bed, her face a postcard of tranquility and loveliness after all our ecstasy.

The damn phone started ringing again, and just from the sound of it, I knew there was an emergency coming my way. No doubt, it was a lawyer thing. I could smell bad news from thousands of miles away. I wished I had remained asleep next to my love goddess instead of getting up with the sunlight. But now my Nostradamus device was operating and my fingers were tingling with anxiety. The incessant ringing from the telephone under the pillow was too much to bear. I had to stop it before Louisa was roused. A little voice inside my head was telling me that this was the end of my love fest with Louisa.

I lifted the pillow and picked up the receiver. "Hello?" I said, my voice sounding weary.

"Allo, Allo, Luke?" said a female voice on a bad connection.

"Yes, it's Luke. Who's this?"

"It's Marina, Luke, can you hear me?"

"Marina! Yes, I hear you! Oh, God, if I had known it was you calling, I would've picked up sooner! I tried to find out what's going on, but no one has a clue over here. How's everything?"

"I'm so sorry to disturb you, Luke," Marina said, her voice full of despair. "But I don't have anyone else to call. I've been trying to reach you all week."

"I was away," I said without a qualm. "But don't worry, Marina, you're not disturbing me. Never. Any news about Vasya?"

"That's why I'm calling! I'm scared, so scared! Time is running out. If we don't find Vasya soon, they'll kill him."

"Marina, slow down. Our connection is not good."

I pushed the red button on my voice recorder and started recording our conversation for future reference.

"Luke, are you there?"

"Yes, Marina, I'm here, go ahead."

"Ok, wait a minute," she said. There were voices in the background and I heard Marina cursing at somebody.

"Marina, I'm here."

"Sorry, Luke, calling isn't easy from here. Listen! My Vasya knows too much. He just knows too much. They'll kill him to cover up. I don't know what else to do."

"He knows too much about what?"

"The KGB people don't want Vasya out because the same people who have been persecuting him for all these years are now supposedly businessmen. They formed companies so that they can sell our natural resources to the West. If Vasya talks about who these people really are, it might jeopardize their reputations and disturb their mega-million profits."

"Okay, I see. I'm not going to let you down, Marina. Nor Vasya. That's a promise. What can I do for you? Tell me how I can help."

"Find Lev, please, Luke! Find Lev! He's in Calais. He got away, I don't know how. But he knows where Vasya is being held. Lev got out without talking to me. And the authorities won't ever tell the truth. Finding Lev is my only hope!"

"Calais, France?" I said, just to be sure. "You mean, Lev is in France?"

"Yes. These days everybody's getting out any way they can. Lev's headed to the UK, then to the US from there. By now, he's probably in one of those migrant camps."

"Okay. What about you, Marina?"

Marina didn't answer me.

"Marina, are you there? I'm calling Nicholas right away, we'll put together all of our resources and I'll find Lev, don't worry. Tell me again when Vasya was arrested?"

I heard other voices calling Marina, then some banging.

"Luke, I have to hang up. Someone is knocking on the front door here. Bye, Luke."

The phone went dead. I held on to the receiver listening to the silence, fuming in my head.

"Motherfuckers," I muttered to myself. "You rotten pieces of shit. Why? Why?"

I felt Louisa behind me, lacing her arms around my waist, embracing me in the far corner of the living room where I was hoping my voice wouldn't awake her. I turned around and gazed into her beautiful, innocent eyes looking back at me. All venting on my part was immediately quashed. I felt a deep warm glow start in the pit of my stomach, radiating through my veins.

I rewound the voice recorder and we listened to Marina together: "Find Lev, please, Luke! Find Lev! He's in Calais. He got away, I don't know how. But he knows where Vasya is being held. Lev got out without talking to me. And the authorities won't ever tell the truth. Finding Lev is my only hope!"

I pressed the stop button on the voice recorder and Marina's voice disappeared.

"That's the woman in Russia you told me about," said Louisa. "You were gentle and caring with her. I'm so proud that you're going to help her. I'm about to cry."

"Look, Louisa, to be perfectly honest, I don't know exactly what I can do."

"There's a man in Calais who is going to help us."

"Us?" I said with disbelief. "This has got nothing to do with 'us.' This is my problem. It's complicated."

"Your problems are my problems, love cat. I'm going with you to France to find this man in Calais."

"I do not want you involved in this thing, Louisa. These people we're dealing with in Russia are monsters."

"I'm going with you," she declared, her voice determined and unshakable. "If you were tracking a polar bear in the Arctic, I'd be right next to you there, too."

Unsure of how to handle this fiery woman, I said nothing and lit a cigarette.

"Look," I finally submitted, "even if I find Lev, and he can tell us where Vasiya is being held, I don't know if I can help him."

"We'll figure out a solution, my love," she said, reading my anxiety. "There are two of us now. I always wanted to make a difference. Now here's my chance. With you. All the way."

We kissed and touched our foreheads together so we could drink in each other's eyes. Her reassurance was like a warm tropical breeze that came out of her heart, dispatching my doubts and lifting me above my own fears.

"Before anybody goes anywhere, I'm calling my friend, Nicholas, and getting him and his Fedpals up to speed."

"I travel light, you'll see," she said.

"We fly tomorrow."

I BOOKED TWO seats to Paris on an Air France flight departing the next day. That night, and again at the crack of dawn before we left for the airport, I called Nicholas. No answer, so I left him a detailed message about Marina's call and my going to France to find Lev.

After we checked our bags, I stopped in a telephone booth in the airport lobby to try Nicholas one more time. Inside that booth at JFK, there was a lot of graffiti scratched, scribbled and tagged everywhere you looked. While they spoke to loved ones, the steady procession of callers had inscribed words like "love" and "freedom" on every available surface. I saw all those tags in a totally different light now, like cries for help from people everywhere struggling to free themselves from oppressive regimes. Freedom and love are the great levelers, uniting everyone around the world.

I finally got Nicholas on the line. He assured me that he had my back with the State Department in Washington and the American Embassy in Paris.

"But Luke," he warned me. "You know about bureaucrats in D.C."

"No, I don't," I said. "They're your friends, not mine."

"They are no one's friends, Luke. They are like the wind, sometimes blowing with you, sometimes against you."

"Tell them we'll need visas and we'll need them fast. And money for tickets, too."

Nicholas was silent for a moment, thinking. I saw Louisa in the airport lobby about 50 feet from the telephone booth, waiting for me, a beautiful smile on her face. She pointed silently at the watch on her wrist. I gave her a thumbs up.

"You know what," Nicholas finally said. "Let's not dance around with these assholes. I'll take care of all the expenses through my firm and arrange housing, then get reimbursed later. Travel safe."

I walked over to Louisa and took her into my arms.

"Nicholas has never met these people. But just on my word, he's willing to get them airline tickets, arrange visas, house them, feed them, take care of them while they get back on their feet in the States. Doesn't that sort of kindness inspire you?"

Without a word, Louisa put her arms around my neck and pulled my face close to hers. She looked at me in silent awe for a long moment.

"You inspire me," she said.

She kissed me deeply, ignoring all the people zigzagging around us.

"They're boarding our flight," I said when our lips parted.

"They won't leave without us, my love."

"Yes, they will. Let's get going. I just hope we're not too late to find Lev."

VASILY'S ARREST WAS high on the KGB's to-do list for a long time. They had been patient, waiting diligently for the right moment to lock him up. The publication of the non-existent dissidents list in *The Washington Post* had given them an opportunity and they seized it without hesitation. Rightly or not, I felt implicated in Vasily's fate.

The *Gebeshniki*[13] arrested him inside his favorite church, the Savior on the Spilled Blood Church, named for Tsar Alexander II who was assassinated in 1881 on that very site. Vasya regularly attended morning prayers there.

Dressed in their standard uniforms of black leather jackets and dark sunglasses, the KGB team strolled into the church that morning with slow, deliberate steps. This evil organization's landmark achievement, its only achievement, was showcasing their absolute power over people, even under the roof of this holy venue. This church was not only a place of worship where people prayed or received communion. It was also a reservoir of peace and tranquility where people sought quiet respite from their otherwise tragic and miserable daily existence. Their vulnerability made the church the perfect place for the KGB to infiltrate people's heads with dark fears about challenging the Communist system and its *apparatchiks*.

Seeing the KGB walk in that morning, Vasya understood that this was the end. He quietly looked up at the gold-covered icon of Jesus Christ on the wall and whispered:

"Father, forgive them, for they know not what they are doing."

---

[13] Slang for KGB.

A cold voice from directly behind Vasya's head whispered: "Not even He can help you, *svoloch*[14].

"You can't arrest me here," said Vasya.

Feeling as if the KGB were tightening a noose around his neck, Vasya jumped up on the church's podium next to the marble altar and screamed out to the other churchgoers:

"The Bolsheviks are an illegal entity in our country! You, the Bolsheviks are occupiers of my motherland at the behest of the international globalist secret societies. Your goal is to destroy Mother Russia and enslave us, so you can have your one world socialistic government. Lenin and Stalin were both mass murderers! Together they killed more than twenty million of our people! They created a cannibalistic society that eats itself in perpetual cycles! I'm not one of you! As a matter of fact, I have nothing in common with you!"

As Vasya continued his cantankerous speech, he noticed that worshippers were quietly moving down the aisles away from the pulpit. Like rats scurrying off a sinking ship, people were clearly terrified. They hurried toward the exits, breaking into a panicky retreat once outside. The eldest who couldn't move that fast decided to hide under pews and behind the altar tables.

"Comrades, Friends, Brothers and Sisters, do not run away, don't be afraid of them! If you all run away, who is going to defend our country and fight these devil- worshipping Luciferians? They are the incarnation of the devil! Look how they're dressed! These people exist by drinking our blood. Come and stand next to me!"

"Are you done, *souka*?"[15] said the commanding KGB officer loudly so everyone in the church could hear him.

Now no one was left in the church, except Vasya and the dozen KGB operatives. The KGB guys stared silently at Vasya with frigid looks of pity and disgust.

"I'm not afraid of you. See, I'm very strong because I am a free man. Do you hear me? I said I am a free man!"

---

[14] Bastard.
[15] Bitch.

"Shut up *gadyuka*[16]," said the KGB officer. "All we have to do is to let you talk. Everyone sees clearly now the poison and hatred you harbor in your heart against our country."

"This is not your country. This is my country. I am an authentic Russian "*mouzhik*[17]. You might be speaking in Russian but you're anything but Russian. You're the lobotomized Praetorian Guard of the Communist Party. Why don't you go ahead and shoot me now? Let's make it easier. Can you give me any sign that I'm actually speaking to a human being? Hey, comrade Captain, can I buy you a smile? One last smile, please."

"If you're pretending that you've gone mad, it won't work this time around, comrade Verbitsky! We have seen you play this game many times before."

"Not this time, comrade Captain. I think I really lost my mind for good. And I'm not even sure if I want it back anymore. It's easier to be a madman in this country than a rational citizen."

"You're on drugs and drunk again, you goddamn alcoholic!" said the KGB officer, then he turned to his crew.

"Get this bitch off of his high chair and put him into the car. We will continue our conversation in Lubyanka[18]. Let's see if he'll make any speeches over there."

The men in sunglasses grabbed Vasya and carried him away while he continued spitting out insults at the government and its agents. The KGB officer was the last one to leave, turning back at the door, calling out to anyone who would listen:

"Where's the damn priest here? Who let this lunatic into church? Are they conspiring with him?"

---

[16] Snake.
[17] Common man.
[18] Famous KGB prison in Moscow.

THE INTERROGATION ROOM deep inside Lubyanka was a dank, gray cubicle whose thick cement walls were discolored from the humidity that relentlessly seeped down from the city's sewers far above. It was so far under the surface of the earth that oxygen was in short supply, making the very act of breathing down there an effort. You could sense the pressure of the entire capital city looming above your head. The ceiling had fine cracks running in every direction, as if, at any moment, the entire prison would come crashing down, crushing Vasya, its sole occupant, under the incomprehensible weight of its steel-reinforced concrete. The silence down there was suffocating as well, the air heavy with apprehension and forced confessions. Imagining all that room's screams, curses and cries of despair from decades of tortured prisoners made Vasya's blood run cold.

That's why Vasily had a terrible headache. He was sitting on the cold floor of the cell with his eyes closed when the rusty door opened. The KGB Captain pushed Lev into the room and entered behind him. Vasya almost didn't recognize Lev because they had beaten him so badly that his face was disfigured and swollen. Blood was still oozing from the wounds on his scalp. Only Lev's eyes were recognizable on his otherwise unrecognizable face. Lev's right hand was bandaged, but the white gauze around his finger had turned bloody red.

"Lyova, what did these animals do to you?"

"They've pulled out one of my fingernails," Lev said, bursting into tears.

"Why?" Vasya turned to the KGB Captain. "Why did you do it? Why?"

"We did nothing to him. But he did something very bad to you. Want to see?"

Without waiting for Vasya to respond, the KGB Captain held out a confession signed by Lev.

"I don't want to read that shit. I don't believe a word of it," said Vasya.

"You call this guy your friend?" said the KGB Captain. "Here's your name in black and white as the leader of a subversive group called Svoboda[19]. And here's your pal's signature. What a name for a group! Who gave it to you? The Americans? Working for the CIA? Svoboda? Really? Freedom from who, asshole? We need freedom from you!"

Vasily glanced at the phony document.

"Lyova, Lyova my dear friend."

"I'm sorry, Vasya," mumbled Lev through swollen lips. "They've forced me."

"I'm not upset with you, Lyova. Don't worry yourself. But what they did to you! It's my fault."

The KGB Captain thrust the confession at Vasily like a sword.

"Of course it's your fault, souka[20]. Now it's your turn. Sign it!"

Vasya suddenly burst into mad laughter.

"Me? You want me to sign that bullshit?"

The sound of Vasya's terrifying laughter echoed off the walls and traveled down the hallway, interrupting the otherwise profound silence of Lubyanka's lowest basement. Even in his pain and misery, Lev understood immediately that Vasya's laughter was his swan song. He grabbed the confession out of Vasya's hands and ripped it in half.

The KGB officer jumped into action, first kicking his black boot at Lev's bandaged hand, knocking the paper out of his grip. Lev screamed in excruciating pain. Then the Captain pinned Lev's bloody bandaged hand to the ground, gradually increasing the pressure with his boot. The pain was unbearable. Lev cried out, his whole body shaking. He looked over at Vasya. Somehow, the two old friends

---

[19] Freedom
[20] Bitch

managed to lock their gazes with one another. Vasya was going mad in front of Lev's eyes. With an enormous act of willpower, Lev tried to capture one final glimpse of Vasya's sanity. As the two men stared into each other's eyes, Lev lost consciousness. A moment later, Vasya was knocked out cold with a powerful blow just above the nape of his neck.

When Vasya opened his eyes next, it was hours later. His head ached, evidently from the big black and blue bruise on the back of his head. The cell was empty. All traces of the KGB Captain and Lev had evaporated. Out of the habitual silence of Lubyanka, Vasya heard heavy footsteps coming down the hallway, approaching the door to his cell. Then a small hatch in the prison door opened and a tray with a bowl of soup was pushed in.

"Hey, Vasya," whispered the prison guard in the hallway. "You've got a letter under the bowl."

Vasya took the tray and put it on the floor, lifting up the tepid bowl of soup. For some unknown reason, the guard was waiting for him to say something in response.

Taped to the underside of the soup bowl was a razor blade.

"Thank you, comrade," said Vasya softly.

He turned and looked through the narrow hatchway, seeing the guard's doleful face watching him. The guard said nothing, but Vasya read "I'm sorry" in the man's eyes.

Vasya stared at the razor blade and looked back at the guard with gratitude. Then the guard's face disappeared as the hatch was shut tight.

Vasya turned his attention to the soup bowl. He carefully picked up the razor blade with his left hand. He paused for a long moment and then squeezed the blade firmly against the artery on the back of his right wrist. The incision released a gush of hot blood that ran out over his hand, then down his thigh, his knees, collecting on the prison floor.

Vasya took a deep breath and used the razor blade higher up on his right arm, slowly cutting the vein wide open. The blood flooded out. Tears rolled down his cheeks, but they were tears of relief. With his fading energy, Vasya looked upward toward the heavens.

"God, this must be how freedom feels."

"I don't know, Vasily. I have never been free Myself."

"God, You're not free?"

"Not at all."

"Burdened by us all?"

"Yes."

"At least I will free You from myself. Remember the Queen song? *This Is Our Last Stand?*"

"I do."

"Welcome me, Father. I'm so tired."

"I'm ready for you, my son."

"Here I come. I'm almost there."

Lost in his thoughts, Vasya switched the razor blade to his bloody right hand and started cutting the veins on the left arm. The blood underneath his feet became deeper and redder.

With each breath, Vasya felt his life slipping further and further away. Finally at the end of that endless road, Vasya held his last breath as long as he possibly could. He had just enough energy to exhale one last time, feeling all the grief and despair, but also all the liberation and peace that comes at the end.

Vasya dropped to the floor, his eyes open wide, gazing at the large pool of his own blood.

LOUISA AND I were driving through the French countryside in a rented Peugeot 405, heading towards the city of Calais. We had landed in Paris only a couple of hours before and decided to take the backroads towards the famous port city situated only 21 miles across the English Channel from Dover. When people talked or wrote about Calais nowadays, it wasn't about the city's rich heritage, or its fine lace industry or its watchtowers, forts and museums, nor about Rodin's famous bronze, *The Burghers of Calais,* standing majestically in front of its town hall.

Sadly, Calais was now referenced as home to "The Jungle," the makeshift camps where the world's disenfranchised and persecuted were holed up in miserable colonies, living a modern, hand-to-mouth version of the Dark Ages. Ripped from their homes and belongings, forced to flee from every corner of the globe, these diverse and incompatible peoples – call them what you will, exiles, emigrants or refugees – shared one common goal: finding a safe place to work and raise their families. Their Golden Fleece was asylum in the UK, where so many others before them had been given the opportunity to re-start their godforsaken lives. They were willing to jump on trucks, grab onto moving trains, sneak onto ferries, anything, no matter the risk to their lives, in order to cross the English Channel to the Promised Land.

On the car radio, French pop star Vanessa Paradis was singing *Be My Baby* with her famous child-like voice, begging her lover never to abandon her. Louisa was asleep next to me in the shotgun seat, her head leaning against the window. I glanced at her catnapping face and the heart-wrenching truth became evident to me: I couldn't live another day of my life without her at my side. We had morphed into one being. All I could think about was pulling off the road into one of the sunflower fields we were passing by, covering her with passionate kisses and joining our bodies into one.

For the first time in my life, I was not in charge of my own destiny. Love was.

With one hand on the wheel and the other on the back of Louisa's neck, I was driving through the postcard-pretty French countryside with the wind whistling in my ears. But I was having a hard time calming the shiver that was racing up and down my spine.

Then as if by magic, a hang glider suddenly spread its wings in my mind and gently lifted my heart up into the sky like a beautiful feather gliding up on the breeze. Somehow I was able to fly up there and simultaneously steer the car from high above the road with a perfect bird's eye view of everything.

Love makes your heart fly. Life is different up here, more luminous, more joyful, far above earthly woes. Now I understand why people who fly away on love never want to land back again.

I was driving now from my vantage up in the air. It seemed as if the car was going where it wanted and I was just following along from high above. With my bird's-eye view, I saw our rented car veering off the road, as if in slow motion, and heading into a field of sunflowers. A moment later, I was back in the driver's seat, braking calmly, bringing the car to a stop in the head-high sunflower plants. I turned to Louisa, who was sitting up and laughing. The car doors opened and she took off through the field, running joyfully like that day at Bear Mountain. Every time we found ourselves in the country, she wanted to run and play. I hurried after her, impatient to hold her in my arms again.

She was up ahead but I couldn't see her through the countless stands of sunflowers. Running hard, I was chased by buzzing bees and dusted by showers of dark yellow pollen from the ripe sunflowers. I somehow got one last glimpse of the scene from on high. The field we were in looked like a single patch of a golden quilt. Suddenly I stumbled on an irrigation pipe and fell down on the moist ground.

Louisa continued running and I was happy for her. I turned onto my back and look up through the towering sunflower plants and tried one last time to imagine myself high up, soaring above everything on my hang-gliding heart. But that vision disappeared in a flash when I heard Louisa's terrifying scream somewhere in front of me.

I jumped to my feet because her scream was anything but playful. It was panicky and aching. I heard a second, more desperate call for help. I started running through the field of sunflowers toward her cries. Something had gone terribly wrong. I came out into an open patch of land bordered by a row of tall cypresses. Louisa was standing next to a ditch at the far edge of the field, sobbing to herself. I walked up beside her and put my arm around her. Her face was frozen in a painful grimace, trembling and unnerved.

She pointed down at the bottom of the ditch where a dead man was lying face up in the mud. I went down there for a closer look. The corpse was covered with flies and mosquitoes. His skin was caramel-colored and his tattered clothes were those of a Middle-Eastern migrant.

"He must've died during the night," I told Louisa. "Sorry you had to see this."

"Please don't touch him," she said.

She motioned for me to get away from the terrible specter of the corpse. When I climbed out of the ditch, she put her arms around my waist and pulled me to her. I hugged her tightly, feeling her shiver uncontrollably. Without exchanging another word, we walked back to the car arm-in-arm and drove away from the field in heavy silence.

As we got back on the road to Calais, we were deadly quiet. The reality of the unfortunate man dying in a ditch far away from his homeland was too much for Louisa to bear. She started crying again, even harder than before. I pulled the car off the road and onto the shoulder, leaving the engine to idle, and took her into my arms. She moaned softly as if she was hurting inside. The private thoughts that were bouncing around inside her mind gushed out in one sobbing confession.

"I don't ever want to die alone," she said.

"You're not dying as long as I'm breathing."

"Just in case it ever happens, don't leave me to do it on my own. I want to have a loved one there with me. Promise!"

"I promise. Now come on, enough crying, please."

"I want to go home. I don't think I can go on."

"Yes, you can. You said you wanted to come with me. We've made it this far, we're not going back without finding Lev and getting him out of this place. I think he's in one of the camps around here. We're close now. C'mon, my love, let's keep going."

"Okay," said Louisa with a long sigh. She paused for a moment to collect her thoughts.

"I'm sorry," she whispered, "for being so weak."

"You're so strong," I said. "My stomach is churning too, but we must go on." I pulled the car out on the road again, though everything seemed darker and more threatening.

"Here we go," I mumbled with a heavy heart. Privately, I wondered if we really were ever going to find Lev.

In a couple of miles, we had to slow down and pass through some sort of temporary police checkpoint. A young gendarme in a smart, starched uniform asked to see our identification. We gave him our passports, which he looked at perfunctorily. Then I showed him my United Nations Office of Oversight card, which got little more than a nonchalant shrug out of him. I asked him where the migrant camps were.

"*Dans la forêt, monsieur*," he said. «*Mais il ne faut pas y aller, au moins pas avec une femme.*»

«*Nous recherchons un ami, un Russe,*» I told him.

The gendarme turned to his colleague and said with well-practiced monotone:

«*Les Americains sont amis avec les Russes, maintenant?!*»

"*Oui, Monsieur,*" I told him. "*Les temps changent.*"

The gendarme told me matter-of-factly that our Russian friend may not have made it to a camp, that he may be one of the dead migrants that local farmers are finding in their fields. Some had died of disease, malnutrition or exposure. A few of them had even committed suicide. There was no emotion on the young man's face, having learned all too well to avoid any expression of sympathy when he was wearing his spiffy French police uniform. I told him about the corpse we'd found near the road a couple miles back. He said they had a special division that took care of "those problems."

"I didn't know you spoke French so well," said Louisa. "What did he say?"

"I told him we're looking for a Russian friend and he made a crack to his partner that Americans are now friends with Russians. I said that times have changed."

"*En effet,*" continued the gendarme with a touch of chagrin. «*Regardez Monsieur, ce temps nouveau, quand moi-même je dois controler les passeports, non pas aux frontiers mais à l'intérieur de mon propre pays.*»

Louisa glanced at me, waiting for me to translate.

"He said that when he has to run a security checkpoint inside his own country, not on a border, it really proves that times have changed."

"Now I wish I hadn't skipped out on my French classes," said Louisa.

I thanked the gendarme and we drove on toward Calais.

"My mother forced me to go to private lessons. She would have killed me if I'd ever skipped out on my tutor."

"Another time I want you to tell me all about your mother."

Suddenly the twinkle was back in her eyes. Her smile was contagious once again.

"Oy, my mother," I replied, smiling painfully at Louisa. "That conversation will require one good bottle of single malt whisky. Neat, no ice please."

"Sure," said Louisa, regaining her spirits. "There may be more resemblance there than you might think."

"Oy," I repeated.

Fortunately just then, I spotted a large campfire through the trees of a thick forest and I was saved from talking about my prickly relationship with my mother. I pulled the car over and parked. Hand-in-hand, we started our search for Lev in this part of "The Jungle."

AS WE WALKED along a muddy road through massive trees that filtered out the day's last sunlight, it was hard to believe that we were only a few miles from a modern European city. Judging by the tracks on the ground, a small bulldozer had carved out that narrow road, clearing away fallen branches so that pick-up trucks could roll through the forest and reach the refugees with supplies. The campfire blazing in a clearing up ahead guided us toward the first of the camps that were tucked away in the forest where the leafy canopy of pines and elms above our heads had turned the sky pitch-black, creating a Kafkaesque landscape. Flames licking sparks upwards from the campfire magnified the atmosphere of doom and hell on earth.

As we came up to the lean-to shacks and patched huts that made up the village, we saw clusters of sub-Saharan Africans, North Africans, Afghans and middle-Easterners. They were mostly young men looking abandoned by their home countries, desperation written on their solemn faces. Many were warming themselves around the crackling campfire. Some were cooking on little gas stoves that must have been donated by the local authorities. Others were lying on cardboard beds, eyes open, exhausted by the burden of their uncertain futures. Women and children were sitting in a tight circle on a plastic tarp spread on the ground, clinging to one another as if the Apocalypse was lurking somewhere out of sight in the surrounding darkness.

No one paid much attention to us as we walked through the camp looking for Lev in a sea of dark, grim faces. Louisa stared wide-eyed at all the refugees, bewildered by her first encounter with this tidal wave of human misery. She was speechless. I could read all the questions bubbling up and reverberating behind her incredulous expression. I wished I could have given her solid answers:

How could this happen in the middle of Europe and people don't know about it, or if they do, even care?

How come this is not front page news every day?

Why are normal people not enraged about all this suffering around the corner from their homes?

Where is the United Nations?

Where is the Red Cross?

Where are all those other humanitarian organizations?

How can we let people live in these conditions?

Who is really helping these lost souls?

Louisa turned to me, narrowing her eyes, unable to speak, deflated and disheartened.

"I don't have the answers," I said. "No one does."

In respectful silence, we left that camp behind and continued down the forest road toward an even larger campfire in a clearing a few hundred yards away. Under a patch of night sky, I stopped and took Louisa into my arms, trying to explain the inexplicable.

"These people are us," I told her. "This is humanity, our humanity. We are all part of the problem. We are all responsible. We can land men on the moon and annihilate each other with nuclear bombs. We are beautiful and monstrous, inspiring and shameful, generous and treacherous. We're human and we can't change human nature."

We kissed under the starlight.

"But we can make a difference," I whispered. "One person at a time. I firmly believe that. It's why we're here and looking for Lev. We are making a difference, you and I, together."

She was overwhelmed, moved to tears. I held her tight.

"I understand," I said, "how hard it is to be a witness to all this agony and go on with our lives, pretending as if nothing had happened."

"Is it a bad time to tell you how much I love you?" she said, drying her eyes. "And how much I admire you?"

"It's the other way around. If you weren't in my life, I probably wouldn't be here now."

"I inspire you?"

"Our love is my fuel. It gives me courage."

She laughed that refreshing, innocent laugh of hers, so unexpected to hear in the midst of all the hopelessness around us. Taking my hand in hers, she kissed my fingers. Then she tugged me forward, having regained her composure.

"The next camp looks bigger," she said, "like it's been here longer."

"More people too," I said.

As we approached, we saw scores of refugees around the campfire. From there, passageways radiated out, lined by multicolored tents made from all kinds of recovered plastic. This camp looked more like a real village, with spray-painted road signs hung on poles with primitive arrows pointing us toward Queen Elizabeth Street, Jungle is Our Home Street, or Black is Not A Crime Street. One entrepreneur had opened his own little commerce, tagging it "Young Afghan's Smoke Shop" on a shingle above the door. On the tin wall of that pop-up shop was a Banksy stenciled image of Steve Jobs wearing a backpack and carrying a vintage Apple computer, like a refugee on the run.

We found the camp's central pathway, called Main Street, and walked along where the most permanent-looking shelters stood. Enticing aromas of spices from around the world rose up from unseen wood stoves. The savory smoke hovered over the shoddy rooftops, mixing with the fog that had seeped into the forest from the English Channel. A gauzy, other-worldly light made the place look post-apocalyptic. It seemed like hundreds of refugees – a kaleidoscope of races and ethnicities – had organized their lives here as if they were the only surviving species of humanity left on Earth after a nuclear holocaust.

At the end of Main Street, we came to a large tin shelter where we heard the voices of many people gathered together, talking animatedly, laughing, exchanging stories in a variety of languages. We paused to listen. The divergent voices floated upwards as if toward the Tower of Babel itself. Suddenly, I heard Lev's unmistakable baritone speaking in English. I silently gestured to Louisa to follow me. Then I pushed open the shack's rag door, bowed respectfully and quickly found a place for us to sit on the plastic tarp floor.

Lev was standing next to a wood stove with a large mug in his left hand, addressing an audience of more than a dozen refugees. He waved around his bandaged right hand, making one of his signature toasts. We were sitting behind him, so he didn't notice me.

"...Somewhere in a forest on an island in the Pacific was a thousand-year-old oak tree," said Lev. "One day, the tree got tired of being a thousand years old. A thousand years of loneliness is too much to bear, even for a tree. 'I'm going to change my name from oak tree to the tree of sadness,' announced the oak tree to all his leaves and branches.

"Nearby, a large family of mice were planning a wedding. Suddenly the wind came up and pushed heavy clouds over the forest. The clouds got scared and they started to cry. Cold rain fell on the forest. The mice gathered all their belongings and climbed up the trunk of the oak tree. Feeling the little mice, the oak tree warmed up from inside. He said to his leaves and branches, 'I'm back into being an oak tree. I'm not alone anymore. Now I can go on another thousand years.'

"Friends," Lev concluded, "Let's drink to the cold rain that forces the mice and the tree to warm up to one another. These are hard times, but if we stick together and look after one another, we will succeed too!"

Lev lifted his mug high and drank down his water in one long gulp. People in the shelter shouted out "Cheers" in a several different languages, raising their mugs, glasses and plastic cups of water to Lev. Meanwhile Lev flipped on a portable radio that started playing out an old Russian folk tune. People stood up, formed a circle and put their hands on each other's shoulders, swaying together, humming along with the tune.

That's when Lev spotted me. At first, he was speechless, blinking his eyes to make sure they were working, and that I wasn't a hallucination. Then his face lit up and he came over to me with his arms open wide.

"Oh, my precious God! Luke? Is that you, my friend? I don't believe my eyes." He hugged me warmly, wiping away a few tears with his bandaged hand. "Is it really you? What are you doing in this crazy place?"

"Looking for you," I said. "Lyova, I'm so happy to find you. Look at you, you're even making toasts."

"But with nothing but water! How did you find me?"

"Marina told me."

"Ah, Marina! I miss her so much now. How is she?"

"I don't know. Last I spoke to her, she was very worried about Vasya. Do you know where he is?"

"Oh, Vasya..." Unexpectedly, Lev broke down and could no longer hold back the tears. "Vasya, Vasya..." he kept saying.

Louisa gently took Lev's bandaged hand.

"Hi Lev, my name is Louisa. We can talk about it later, no? Do we need to change this bandage?"

"No, that's nothing," Lev said, wincing in pain but waving her off. "So nice to meet you, Louisa. There's not much I can offer you here. You didn't even bring any Stoly, did you? Ah, just a bad joke. They've got nothing but water to drink here!"

"Lev, we came to get you out. We need to move."

"Move?"

"You're coming with us."

"Where to?"

"The United States Of America."

"But how?"

"We've made all the arrangements, but we don't have much time. Pack your stuff and let's go."

Lev was in total disbelief. But he hadn't lost his sense of humor.

"Pack what stuff?" he said. "I'm wearing my suitcase!"

EARLY THE NEXT morning, we were sitting blurry-eyed inside a sleek café in Terminal 2F at Paris' Charles De Gaulle Airport, watching travelers come and go with their luggage and colorful clothes. People from all over the world hurried by us, well-dressed, well-fed, and, as the French say, comfortable in their own skin. It was light years away from the "Jungle" camps we had come from.

We were numb.

The night before I had driven down the A-1 highway from Calais, pulling off the road for snacks at a truck stop. After we ate, Louisa and I curled up in the front seat for a nap while Lev stretched out in the back for some much-needed rest. Before dawn, we arrived at the airport, dropped off the rental car and caught a shuttle to Terminal 2C.

Now, the three of us were inside this modernistic terminal sitting on barstools at the Columbus Café and looking like sad, tired birds forced to make an emergency landing en route to milder climates. The awful camps were behind us, but we couldn't shake the feelings that the camps had engendered. Our clothes still smelled of the immigrants' exotic spices, a constant reminder of the heart-wrenching reality we had just witnessed. Our spirits felt sucked dry, as if the camps were like a malignant cancer that had somehow metastasized inside of us, ravaging all hope and desire.

Waiting to board our flight, we sipped green tea and espressos in this peaceful corner of the busy airport, physically here, but thinking about all the people with broken lives stuck in limbo back in the war zone outside Calais. Lev finally spoke up, jolting us back to the here and now.

"This café is named after the man who discovered America," he said. "I'm about to do the same."

Louisa and I didn't respond. We glanced at one another and turned back to Lev, both proud, nodding our agreement.

"I know I should be happier right now," Lev continued. "But I'm not. Just like the way you need friends to share the bad times with, you also need friends to share the good times with. Otherwise, nothing makes sense."

Lev put his bandaged hand on my shoulder.

"This might sound very strange to you, Luke, but I feel free for the very first time in my life. And at the same time, I feel so lonely. I can say whatever I like without fear of the authorities. But I am all alone. It is a paradox, isn't it? Maybe life is just about confronting one paradox after another?"

"Lev," Louisa said, "coming out of the Soviet Union, going through the Jungle, now off to the United States, you need to give yourself time to find your way. Your journey wasn't easy. But you're going to a good place now."

She squeezed Lev's arm with both her hands. No words could describe the gentle sweet love I saw pouring out of her hands like a wellspring. All I could think about was kissing each of her hands, embracing each of her graceful fingers.

"I miss Marina and Vasya," said Lev. "This journey does not make any sense to me without them. I have spent all my adult life with them. I was the one who introduced them at university. Marina was my classmate. We fought the Soviets together, we partied together, we got drunk together, we vacationed together. I miss them. I miss them so much."

Lev started crying softly.

In the midst of the airport's organized chaos, we were sitting in an emotional bubble, impervious to all the travelers swirling around us. Louisa and I couldn't find the words to console Lev, an imposing man who now seemed small and pale, his body trembling. We silently watched Lev wipe his eyes dry with his bandaged hand. I finally found my own voice, looking to change the mood.

"What happened to your hand, Lev?"

The question made Lev choke on the coffee he was sipping, spilling a little down the front of his shirt. But the tears were gone, and his natural cheekiness came back.

"This?" he said, waving his bandaged hand in the air. "It's bullshit! That's what you guys say in America when something is a lie, right? Bullshit? Well, this is Soviet bullshit, KGB-style."

Louisa and I glanced at each other.

"What happened?"

"A going-away gift from the KGB," said Lev. "The interrogator pulled my fingernail out."

"Oh no!" Louisa groaned.

Lev shuddered, took a deep breath and continued, "Oh, yes, it was the most horrible pain I've ever experienced.

I blacked out and thought I had died. But I survived it, just like I got through all the rest of their humiliating techniques. And now I'm so happy to be here with you. There's hope again in my life."

Lev gave us a big smile. But Louisa shot me another distressful look. I put my hand on Lev's shoulder and looked hard into his eyes, showing my alarm.

"Lev, you should've told me about this before. We could have gone by a hospital. Why didn't you?"

"I didn't want anything," he said, "to get in the way of our road to freedom."

"Lev, listen to me, this is a crime punishable under the United Nations Convention Against Torture. We need to document this with a doctor as soon as we arrive in the States and file a lawsuit against the perpetrators. Can you identify them? Can you name names?"

Lev smiled and shook his head.

"My friend, you are so naïve," he said. "Don't get me wrong, you and your lady friend are the kindest and most gentle souls I have ever met. But you have no idea who you're dealing with here. You think these people give a damn about the United Nations or any nice conventions about torture? Who's going to hold them responsible? Who? Nobody will!"

"No," I said determinedly, "we will hold them responsible. We won't let them get away with this."

"Oh, Luke," said Lev with a trembling voice. "You're so naïve. I'm just happy I am out of that black hole."

Louisa silently stood and gave Lev a hug. Lev held her gratefully. When their embrace ended, I said:

"I'm sorry for what you went through, Lev, but it's over. You're safe now. We'll do everything in our power so you can have a normal life going forward. You deserve it."

"A normal life? I can never have a normal life. Not anymore. I'm sorry to always give you guys my bad news. When you say everything is possible, I say it's impossible. When you say, 'Don't worry, it's going to be okay,' I say, 'Nothing will be okay.'" Where you see happy stuff, I see nothing but gloom and doom. You Americans are such optimists, and we are such…"

Suddenly unable to express himself, Lev covered his face with his hands and started sobbing again. We silently waited for the storm to pass. His weeping seemed to burst from a deep and ancient well of anguish and fear, each teardrop finally releasing years of amassed repression.

"…We Russians are such goddamned pessimists," he managed to say, wiping his eyes dry.

On the PA system in the café, Alain Souchon's song, *Foule Sentimentale,* came up softly.

Lev evidently felt better after his crying spell. "I'm sorry for bawling like a baby," he said. "I don't know what came over me." He paused to listen to the music on the PA system.

"I love Alain Souchon. We used to listen to him in Vasya's apartment and imagine that we were walking along some cobblestone street in Montmartre. Do you guys listen to Alain Souchon?"

Louisa and I looked at each other with a shrug.

"We don't know him," I said.

"Do you know any other French singers?" Lev asked.

"Besides Charles Aznavour and Edith Piaf?" said Louisa. "Not really."

Lev had a surprised look on his face.

"Henry Miller said America is a cultural desert, no?"

"Lev, he also said that living in the United States is an air-conditioned nightmare."

"Is that true?"

"It's Henry Miller, Lev. You can't take him seriously. When he lived in Paris, his sole purpose was getting into Anais Nin's panties. She was a sex-bomb. He'd say and do anything just to have her. He wrote with his dick. And he was damn good at it!"

Louisa laughed.

"Lev, here's a secret," I continued. "If you want to be appreciated by French intellectuals, start bashing Americans. Especially those who live on the Left Bank. It's a national sport and Henry Miller understood that."

"Is it because they're all leftist-socialists?"

"Yes."

"That's something we never understood in Soviet Union. Don't people see what that vile ideology did to the people in the USSR?"

"They say that the USSR was not real socialism. They say it was a bad experiment."

Lev launched into an eloquent tirade for us and anyone in the Columbus Café to hear.

"How many such bad experiments before those pseudo intellectuals wake up to the fact that a society based on individual rights is the only one where a human being can live free? Have people never read Locke or Jefferson about freedom? Are they really trapped in Karl Marx's demonic views about the future of mankind?

"My friends, you must know this: Karl Marx hated everybody and everything. Vasya and I studied all his published articles. Have you ever read any of them? Marx and Friedrich Engels published their own magazine called *Rheinische Zeitung*. As early as 1849, Marx wrote that when the class war happens, there will be primitive societies that are not capitalist yet, like Basques, Serbs, Scottish highlanders and all Slavic people. He called them 'racial trash.' He said they are two stages behind in the historical struggle, so they must perish in the coming 'revolutionary holocaust.'

"Marx and Engels were the first people to advocate racial extermination. Marx is the forefather of modern political genocide, and still, so-called intellectuals around the world worship him and long for a society based on his ideals?

"It's exactly what happened in the USSR. All Marx's ideas came to fruition, including racial extermination. Lenin and Stalin deported, exiled and murdered entire nations. People have to finally wake up!"

Lev was breathing fire now, speaking with singular passion.

"If you are not free, you cannot experience the gift of life in its fullness. Period. With collective ownership of property, all incentives for working hard and accomplishing anything just vanish. The idea behind 'Collective Goods' is that everyone has equal abilities. But we are not born equal. Everything has to be based on natural law. Some of us are hard workers, but others are lazy. Some are honest, others are thieves. You can't put them all in one basket and ask them to share the fruits of their labor. They have not worked equally or contributed in the same way. Everyone must create his or her own personal journey of growth. And benefit from it accordingly. And for that, you have to be free. Unlike equality, liberty is natural! We are all born free!"

Louisa put her hand on Lev's shoulder to get him to lower his voice. He nodded his head and continued in almost a whisper.

"Unelected bureaucrats start regulating labor and property for their own good. They become the de-facto ruling class. If you're not part of their 'nomenklatura,' the administration, then you live like a serf with no rights. You become their slave.

"Look at East Germany, North Korea, Vietnam or China. Whatever they call themselves – communist or socialist – it makes no difference, people live under autocratic regimes that are run by *apparatchiks*. There are no individual rights, they have no viable economy, and they enforce authoritarian thought control from top to bottom.

"It's easy to live in Europe, consume all the goods that your hard-working ancestors have created for centuries, and advocate a communistic/socialistic la-la-land that does not and will never exist. However, it's a poisonous dream. All it leads to is destruction, poverty, Gulag camps and death. At least 100 million people have been killed by Communist regimes. Maybe more. Socialism is not about the redistribution of wealth, like many leftists think. Socialism is about consolidation of power! History has proved it! I want freedom! I want to make my own decisions about how to live my life!"

People at surrounding tables in the café were staring at us. Lev lowered his voice even more.

"I apologize for being so loud," he said. "We are talking about things that are very close to my heart. We fought for freedom and people died for it. It is hard to explain to others what it was like. But everyone is entitled to his or her own opinion. Who am I to judge? I know nothing. I'm pathetic. Just look at me, a man with no home, no country and no family. I am so pathetic!"

Lev took a deep breath and had another cough attack.

"Let's stop talking politics," said Louisa, "and focus on making sure that Lev is feeling better, okay?"

I took her hint and added my own closure.

"I'm with you, Louisa. Fuck the politics and the politicians. What good ever came out of them anyway? Lies, lies and more lies."

Lev was drained, suddenly wordless.

Just then, thankfully our flight was announced. In no time we were up in the air heading back home.

53

SOMEWHERE OVER THE Atlantic, I found the right moment to break the good news to Lev. All three of us had slept through the take-off and the jet's steep ascent into the clouds. Now we were awake and a little refreshed. Through the plane's windows on either side of the cabin, we caught a glimpse of the blue, sun-dappled Atlantic Ocean stretched out from one horizon to the other. A friendly steward came along the aisle with his moveable cart and served Lev a couple of miniature bottles of vodka with a glass full of ice cubes. Louisa and I ordered fruit drinks.

"I've got a surprise for you, Lev," I said, standing up once the steward had moved past our row.

I got my backpack out of the overhead bin, and sat back down. I pulled out an official-looking envelope and handed it to him.

"From the American Embassy of Paris?" Lev said, looking at the return address. "For me?"

"Open it."

"What is it?" Lev seemed caught off-guard.

"You'll see!"

Lev opened the envelope and found inside his Authorization for Permanent Residency in the United States of America. In the space after "Reason for Refuge," the document said: "Political Exile"

"Oh my God, it's for Mr. Lev Horowitz. No more comrade bullshit."

"The Embassy had a courier bring it to us when we landed in Paris, before we drove to Calais to look for you. Our friend Nicholas made good on his promise. He's also got all the papers ready for

Vasya and his family. It's only a matter of time. We are talking just a few more weeks."

Lev's mouth dropped open, though he didn't speak. He suddenly looked disoriented and gloomy.

"I thought you would be happy," I said.

Lev took a deep breath and composed himself, finally rewarding us with a little forced smile.

"Luke, you always appear out of nowhere to help us. Thank God there are people like you in this world."

"Well, I wasn't much help last time around."

"You gave us hope. And that was so important."

Lev undid his seat belt and stood up abruptly.

"I'm feeling a little nauseous. Be back soon."

I turned and watched him making his way down the aisle and toward the rear of plane, then disappear inside one of the airplane's restrooms. A couple of minutes went by.

Louisa and I exchanged a silent look of apprehension.

"Maybe you should go check on him?" said Louisa.

"I think you're right."

I got down the aisle and stood vigil outside Lev's restroom door, letting a steady stream of other passengers pass me by.

"Just waiting for my friend," I said over and over.

A couple of minutes went by and still there was no sign of Lev. Finally, I knocked on the door and moved close to say:

"Lev, are you okay in there? Lev?"

Without warning, the bathroom door opened abruptly and Lev reached out, grabbed me by my wrist and pulled me into the bathroom with him. Then he quickly slammed the door shut and locked it. There was so little space in there that our faces were almost touching one another.

"Luke, I didn't want to talk about Vasya in front of your lady. It's too gruesome."

"Gruesome?"

"Yes, after you visited us, Vasya decided never to compromise anymore. He wanted to study law and become a human rights lawyer, inspired by you. But the KGB had different plans for us. They were going to arrest us all anyway, even if you had managed to publish the real dissident's list. I knew it. Vasya knew it, too."

"They tricked me, those sons-of-bitches," I said. "I never figured that they had found your list inside my boot and replaced it with their fake list."

"You're new to this game, Luke, they've been at it for the last seven decades."

"At least you got out."

"Vasya warned me all hell was about to break loose. That was just before he burned down that ridiculous Marx-Engels-Lenin poster on Liteyniy Prospect."

"What did he do?"

"He set that damn poster on fire. It was gigantic. Everyone in the city hated the damn thing. It was an ugly reminder of our history. There they were, Marx, Engels and Lenin, all together, the so-called 'founders of the proletarian dictatorship'. What bullshit! We called it the three-headed hydra. It was fantastic when Vasya made it disappear. The fire was all over the news. It was a big scandal for the authorities. Then of course they arrested us all."

"Where is Vasya now, do you know?"

"We were in Lubyanka together. However, I think they took him to a "*psychoushka.*"

"Like a mental asylum?"

"Yes. In our country when you speak the truth, they assume that you must be mentally ill. So they send you to a *psychoushka.* Then you're really screwed."

With our noses almost touching, I could feel Lev's hot breath with every word and smell the vodka. He was sweating profusely and his lips were trembling.

"They arrested Anatoly, too. The KGB beat him up so bad, I think they punctured his lung."

"Bastards," I murmured furiously. "They're sick, cruel people."

"Yes, they're sick and cruel. And very smart. Way too smart. They've managed to stay in power for 70 years now by perfecting the art of intimidation right down to the last, tiny detail.

"Here I am flying with you to freedom, a free man finally, but I can't relax, not for even one moment. I'm afraid. I'm afraid that somehow they are going to make this plane turn around or force it to make an emergency landing, and then burst in, handcuff me and take me back to Lubyanka. I know it sounds irrational, but that's what fear is. I can't explain it. Maybe I've lived with fear far too long and now it has taken root inside my head and won't go away."

"No one is going to stop you from getting to the States," I said.

"Speaking to you calms my nerves, Luke. But I don't want to upset your lady friend. Anatoly told me in the prison that they had already started injecting Vasya with a decoder."

"What's a decoder?"

"It's a powerful medication called Haloperidol."

"Yeah, Vasya told me about that stuff."

"They tell you it's going to balance your moods. But it really kills your short-term memory, with the side effect of causing Parkinson's Disease. And if that doesn't work, then they take you to 'Farming.'"

"Farming?"

"That's exactly what they call it. 'Farming.' They farm you out, turn you into a vegetable. A few injections of psychedelics mixed with toxins and God knows what else, sometimes even radioactive elements. If that doesn't kill you, it transforms your brain into a vegetable. You have no more free will left, nor any sense of your own self. You're better off dead."

"Awful, awful, awful…"

"Now do you understand why I feel so guilty. Why I'm not celebrating this wonderful gift you've given me? I'm here with you, but my mind and heart are with Vasya."

"Does Marina know any of this?"

Lev shook his head.

One of the airline hostesses knocked on the door and asked discretely if there was a problem.

"Thank you, we're fine!" I called out. "Coming out now!"

"No, I didn't give Marina any details. I'm afraid it would kill her. She has suffered enough. When they released me, I called her and told her that I was leaving for France, trying to get to England. I lied and said Vasya would be released and follow me very soon."

"Let's go back to our seats. Louisa is no doubt getting worried."

"Of course," said Lev, adding, "By the way, I have a cousin in America. Her name is Masha Horowitz and she lives in Brighton Beach. She has a bakery there. I was able to call her from Calais. She said I can stay with her family. And I can work in their bakery. I want to live there until Marina comes over."

"And Vasya?" I asked.

"Oh, my dear Vasya…" Lev murmured hopelessly.

54

EVEN IF YOU'VE seen it a thousand times before, the New York City skyline with the Statue of Liberty jutting out of the bay at the foot of Manhattan are landmarks that never cease to provoke wonderment and admiration. As the airplane approached the airport, I saw the city out the airplane's window and spotted the golden torch held on high by Lady Liberty, shimmering in the sunlight. New York City was a goddess who had been offering sustenance to the world's immigrants for over two centuries. She had provided food, shelter and encouragement to millions of pilgrims who arrived on these shores in search of freedom and opportunity. Many fell in love with her and stayed. Others moved on to settle in communities across the country. Each man, woman and child received a little bit of her unfathomable love.

I love New York, the mother city. She's sacred to me. Coming back here was always inspiring. Nevertheless, I felt like the prodigal son who never really comes home. A stabbing fear gripped my gut as soon as the plane touched down, its wheels screeching painfully when their rubber hit the runway. Why the trepidation? Why did I feel at home and yet so far away at the same time? How could I be so at peace here and at war somewhere else, all at once?

Some philosopher said that contradictions are still points where opposites converge. My life, with all my doubts, self-destructive tendencies and self-awareness, was in need of constant re-alignment. Otherwise, I'd lose my sense of being completely alive. So why all the turbulence, both inside and out? Why the continuous questioning? I sincerely felt at one with the world. And the world was at war with itself. I was conflicted too because I wanted to make this world a better place and make myself feel useful. I had to live with those contradictions.

As the airplane taxied toward our gate, I came to an agreement with myself. I wouldn't give up fighting for peace even if that meant going to war. That would be where my opposites converged, my contradictions.

I glanced over at Lev and saw him also thinking about the past and the future, trying to put all his own contradictions into some order as he embarked on his American journey. Our eyes met and I knew that, just like me, he was thinking about Vasya, Marina and their child. I now felt responsible for their fates. I had implicated myself morally and emotionally into their lives. Helping them meant making the world a better place. Helping them made me feel worth-while. I was not stopping now. I was in all the way. And because of me, Louisa was in as well. That was the most worrisome part of the equation.

When we exited customs at the airport, Lev's cousin, Masha, was waiting for us. She was a tall young woman with short brown hair and piercing blue eyes. At the sight of Lev, she burst into tears and took him into her arms for a long, deep, wordless hug. Louisa and I turned away to give them their privacy in the middle of all the other families welcoming loved ones.

Before we went on our way, I glanced back at Lev where decades of frustration, longing and concern were chiseled into his face. Lev grabbed me by the shoulder, turned me to face him and looked into my eyes with gratitude. We agreed to meet in the Washington D.C. offices of Nicholas's law firm as soon as an appointment could be arranged.

"Welcome to your new home, Lev," I said.

"I love you both very much," Lev said, kissing me on my lips, his voice still wavering with emotion.

Masha embraced and thanked both of us. Then she and Lev turned and walked off, embarking on a new chapter in their lives.

55

A FEW DAYS later, late at night, the telephone literally rang off the hook. When I finally picked it up, I heard Nicholas' warm voice calling from D.C., saying he had set up the appointment in two weeks time to review Lev's immigration status. I called Masha who said she would drive Lev down to D.C. for the meeting. Louisa and I would catch the Acela at Penn Station.

Those first two weeks of freedom had transformed Lev. The man who walked into reception area with Masha at Hartman, Cooper & Stein on the 7th floor of the Tower Building at 1401 K Street was healthy, groomed and jocular. Lev was wearing tight-fitting denims with a Barbour jacket. He could have passed for a college professor. The gauntness had been replaced by a well-nourished rosiness. His finger was still bandaged, but more discreetly. Most noticeably, Lev was smiling non-stop. His good humor required an effort to get used to. Louisa couldn't take her eyes off of him, making funny faces at him and giggling when he made faces back at her.

Built in 1929, the Tower Building was one of the first Art Deco structures in D.C. One entire wall of the lobby was a floor-to-ceiling image of Tamara De Lempicka's 1931 masterpiece "Woman with Dove," as if to reinforce the art deco theme of the building's architecture.

Lev was staring at the De Lempicka image as he sipped the steaming espresso that the young receptionist had served him. Masha, Louisa and I chatted about Lev's new life with her family. Nicholas came out to greet us, shook Lev's bandaged hand carefully with both his hands and said with a wide smile on his face:

"Lev, I'm thrilled to see you here today. Please excuse the delay in our getting together."

"Thank you, Nicholas, for everything," said Lev. "Feeling free is the strangest thing. I'm still getting used to it."

We were escorted into an elegant conference room with big windows. When we were seated in the high-backed, leather chairs around an oval table, Lev spoke first:

"Thank you again for what you, Luke and Louisa did for me. I wouldn't be here without all of your efforts."

"You're very welcome, Lev," said Nicholas. "We've always been great admirers of yours and of Vasily Verbitsky and of all the other dissidents. We hated the Cold War. Our idea was to help people re-start democracy in Russia, so we could all live in peace. We all know democracy requires democratic laws and democratic institutions. People needed to be trained to foster everything that Russia was lacking. That kind of mentoring, as you know, was a beloved project of our law firm. But after a lot of effort by people like Luke, we gave up on that strategy. It didn't work."

"Sadly no," said Lev. "The psychological impact of the prison system is still very much alive with our people. You can't be free if you don't have a law-abiding society. The government must also obey the law. Otherwise there's anarchy. The collapse of the USSR was a golden opportunity for security services to take control of our country."

"Which they did."

"Definitely."

"For that reason," said Nicholas, "we are now helping dissidents like you to get out because your lives are as much in danger these days as during the Brezhnev or Andropov eras."

"Maybe even more so."

"Which brings me to the next step, Lev."

Nicholas looked straight into Lev's eyes.

"Lev, how can we get Vasya out of the prison or the asylum, wherever he is still incarcerated?"

"We can't."

"What do you mean?"

"Only Tractor can do it."

"Who's Tractor?"

"The man who expelled Luke and gave orders for them to torture me while I was interrogated. They call him Tractor because during those interrogations, his men would beat you up so badly, you'd feel as if a tractor had run over you. After a session with Tractor, you're an invalid, either physically or mentally. I was lucky to escape with just a little finger problem."

Smiling, Lev held up his right hand to show us his bandaged index finger.

"Tractor thought I could give them more valuable information so he let me keep breathing. Luke got a taste of Tractor as well."

"What's his real name?" I asked.

"His real name is Igor Kravtsov. He's a KGB Colonel. You just don't want to mess with him."

"Where is he now?"

"I heard from some Russians in Brighton Beach that Kravtsov lives in Manhattan now."

"What?" Nicholas and I said simultaneously.

"How is that possible?" asked Louisa, as shocked as we were.

"Some of Kravtsov's old colleagues have also been spotted here. They are in London too. And Hong Kong, I hear. In fact, they show up wherever big money is. The KGB, the German Stasi, the Romanian Securitate, the Polish SB or the Bulgarian Darjavna Sigournost, they have all re-packaged themselves. They call themselves businessmen nowadays. Believe it or not, everyone in the world is willing to do business with them. They are more powerful now than ever before. They're like feudal kings that make their own laws. Do you think they really care about democratic ideas, Nicholas?"

"How do you know about this?" I asked.

"Vasya told me," said Lev. "He knew about everything that was going on. He had researched it. He knew people high up. The first thing he was going to do when he got to Europe was write a book exposing the bullshit with the facts. You know, name names, tell the real story. These businessmen are looting us in broad daylight!"

"What kind of businesses?" asked Nicholas.

"They sell gold, diamonds, oil, gas, liquid gas, military hardware. Everything. You name it, they sell it. All the natural resources of our mother Russia are on sale. They will launder your money and at the same time recruit you for their dirty work if they can. They have government protection because they buy politicians."

"So they think they're immune here as well?"

"Of course," said Lev with a wave of his hand.

"Let's find Kravtsov," I said. "And convince him to get Vasily released."

"Convince Tractor? That's crazy," Lev replied.

"Maybe so," I said. "But this is America, where we don't bow to tyrants, where there are laws against the kind of trafficking you're describing. If not you and me, Lev, who is going to stand up for Vasya?"

Nicholas jumped in. "I don't want anybody going after anyone without me speaking to the authorities first. Is that clear? We need to bring in the FBI on this."

"Go after Tractor?" said Lev. "No way."

"Why not?"

"You don't know these people, Nicholas. You don't know what they're capable of. Especially Tractor. He would eat your FBI for breakfast. He has already eliminated almost all of his competition. Let me tell you a story, a true story about Tractor that Vasily told me."

We all sat in rapt silence as Lev began:

"There was a professor, Professor Stoyanov, a Bulgarian dissident, who was living in the States. He was in Massachusetts. He taught political science in Boston at prestigious universities. Through his contacts, Stoyanov got hold of all the archives of dissidents from the Eastern bloc countries, including the ones in Soviet prisons. All the records of the fake crimes the dissidents were accused of and the real crimes committed against them by KGB, Stasi, Securitate etc.

"He had proof of this modern-day Gulag Archipelago for today's political prisoners, mostly human rights activists. But even more interesting, Stoyanov also got his hands on official records of businesses that the oligarchs had created as sleeper cells for the KGB.

"Stoyanov had made a deal with an important American magazine to publish an article about everything he knew, based on the evidence he had put together. He was waiting for one last envelope containing essential documents coming from his friend, Mykola Chichniak, an Ukranian novelist who had spent 20 years between Moscow's Lyubianka and Matroskaya Tishina prisons.

"The day that Chichniak's envelope was going to be delivered to Stoyanov's peaceful, suburban home, a man on a motorcycle caught up with the postman's truck on an empty street and shot the postman between the eyes. Then the motorcyclist put on the postman's uniform and switched out the envelope addressed to Stoyanov for another one that had a bomb in it. The assassin personally delivered the letter bomb to the Professor. When it exploded, it not only instantly killed Stoyanov, but also set his house on fire. As the postman's van drove away with the assassin at the wheel, the Professor's place was consumed in flames, destroying all his research.

"The story doesn't end there. A few miles away, as the assassin was about to get back on his motorcycle, a black Mercedes-Benz appeared out of nowhere. It plowed into the motorcycle and killed Assassin 1. When Assassin 2 stepped out of the Mercedes to make sure Assassin 1 was dead, Assassin 3 sped by in a BMW and shot Assassin 2 through the heart with one bullet. The story of Assassin 3 ended there because he disappeared, knowing very well that he was going to get killed by his boss.

"The boss of this criminal network was Valentina Sadikova, a 25-year KGB veteran and a real spymaster. She was known by her nickname, *Instrumentalchik*. She had been planted many years ago in a sleeper cell. She was activated through a KGB program called Code 28.

"Sadikova had a front company, a flower shop on a cobblestone street in Greenwich Village. The following day according to eyewitness accounts in the flower shop, no one heard anything unusual. But one customer saw a tiny hole appear in the front door and then Valentina Sadikova dropped to the floor like a sack of wet dirt, a bullet hole where her right eye had been.

"Some say it was the Assassin 3 who killed his own boss. And behind all these murders was "Tractor." He had carried out a false flag operation inside the KGB to take over all the money-making operations. So now you have both Tractor and a rogue expert assassin on the loose. Who wants to deal with them? No one!"

"We never hear those stories here," Nicholas said.

"Of course!" said Lev. "All you hear in America is 'Gorbachev, Gorbachev,' or 'Gorby,' right? The supposed new savior of Russia? It's disgusting."

Lev's voice was trembling with distaste.

"It's true. There is some kind of Gorbamania here," I said.

"Well, you have to know the truth! Gorbachev did everything in his power to save the USSR so that he could save his dictatorship. However the KGB out-maneuvered him. That's why he's so bitter."

"All of this sounds more like a detective novel than reality," said Louisa.

"I wish it was fiction," Lev said, "but believe me, it's real."

A few moments of heavy silence filled the room.

"But we have to help Vasya," I said. "We can't give up on him, can we? Lev, are you with us or not?"

"I would like to take some fresh air," said Lev. "If you don't mind?"

"Yes," said Nicholas. "Good idea. Let's get some lunch and get back together this afternoon."

56

MASHA, LEV, LOUISA and I walked down K Street toward a restaurant a couple blocks away that Nicholas had recommended. Lev silently smoked a cigarette as he walked along, lost in his own thoughts.

Louisa pulled me aside on the sidewalk.

"You're too harsh on him," she said softly.

"I'm too harsh on him? I'm trying to figure out how to help Vasya."

"But Lev's still getting adjusted to life here, there's a lot on his mind. There's so much to sort out."

"I just want to do something while we still have time," I explained. "Nicholas is getting Marina and Vasily's child out so that the KGB doesn't get a chance to blackmail him with that too. Now we need to somehow convince this Tractor character to cooperate with us."

"I understand, my love," said Louisa. "But Lev may not be ready to make any more sacrifices. He wants to enjoy his new life."

"Okay, you're probably right, we have to give him more time."

We had a light lunch and chatted about everything except Vasya, everyone avoiding the subject diplomatically. The meeting that afternoon with Nicholas focused only on Lev's immigration process and the various steps he needed to take on the road to becoming a bonafide U.S. citizen. Nothing else was said about Vasya, but I couldn't stop thinking about him or Tractor.

We bid Nicholas goodbye and left the offices of Hartman, Cooper & Stein later that afternoon. Once we were back on the street, Lev told us there were some Washington sites that he had only read about in books and always wanted to see with his own eyes.

"Let's take a walk," said Louisa.

We strolled toward the Capitol, went down the National Mall past the Washington Monument encircled by American flags and elm trees. As we walked alongside the reflecting pool, Lev became more animated, pointing out the Jefferson Memorial in the distance and singing the praises of the great man who authored the Declaration of Independence.

"Remember what Jefferson said, Luke?" said Lev.

"Yes, I do."

Together we said, "The tree of liberty must be refreshed from time to time with the blood of patriots and tyrants."

At the end of the Mall, we reached the Lincoln Memorial. Lev stopped and looked up at its monumental columns and white façade, smiling like a kid in a candy store. He almost ran up the broad stone stairs of that temple of democracy and disappeared inside the Memorial's great hall. Masha, Louisa and I followed him up the stairs, but we lingered outside, allowing Lev his private time to gaze up at the enormous seated sculpture of our 16th president and re-read Lincoln's speech at Gettysburg that's engraved in stone.

At the top of the Memorial's steps, we enjoyed the cool evening air and the impressive view of the Capitol in the distance, now glimmering with lights. Finally Lev emerged. He looked rejuvenated, his eyes sparkling, a big smile on his face, a spark in his step. He walked up to us, repeating again and again Lincoln's famous words:

"…that government of the people by the people for the people shall not perish from the earth."

The four of us stood close together, silently recognizing this magic moment.

"Friends," said Lev finally. "I apologize for my moment of weakness back at Nicholas' office. Of course I'm going to do everything necessary to help Vasya."

I looked at Louisa with a sigh of relief and took Lev into my arms in a bear hug. Louisa and Masha joined in, the four of us now arm-in-arm at the top of the Lincoln Memorial, laughing and crying together, our embrace uniting our destinies for better or for worse.

"I will never be able to thank you enough," said Lev.

"We're not finished yet, Lev," I said. "There's more work to do."

"I am with you," said Lev firmly. "But how will it all end, what's the next chapter of my Russian-American story?"

AS I WAS driving out of the Holland Tunnel into Manhattan before sunrise, now ten years later, torrential rain turned my windshield into a waterfall. The car's wipers were swishing back and forth as best they could, but the powerful storm was winning the battle, making it tough to see the sparse traffic on rain-soaked Canal Street. At that hour, only garbage trucks and delivery vans were out in the stormy weather.

After driving all night, my eyes looked drowsy in the car's mirror. I pulled over and turned off my engine, enjoying the spectacle of lightning bolts slicing through the dark clouds above the skyscrapers. I closed my eyes and listened to the rain pounding the car like thousands of little hammers, interrupted by occasional cracks of thunder.

Ten years before, the night Louisa and I returned from D.C., a similarly powerful storm had broken over the Bronx. I couldn't sleep that night either. Similarly ruthless rain poured down back then as well, accompanied by loud, ferocious thunderbolts.

It was the perfect soundtrack to my thinking incessantly that night about Lev, Marina, Nicholas and Tractor and what had to happen next. Startled by the commotion outside, Louisa awoke, putting her naked arms and legs around me and snuggling her head under my chin. I heard her sweet voice whispering, as if reading my thoughts:

"I know how much you want to help your dissidents, darling, but you can't take matters into your own hands. Really, you can't."

"Who else is going to act?" I said.

"What if these people are as bad as Lev says they are? It's too dangerous."

"If we get scared of them and do nothing, they win."

"Let the authorities do their work."

"And just observe from the sidelines? Get on with my life and pretend that nothing happened? That Marina didn't call me and ask for help? That Vasya isn't in jail or an asylum? That I never went to Russia and befriended these people? Tell me what you think I should do?"

"Don't get agitated with me," she said, staring at me with love in her sleepy eyes.

"Sorry, my darling," I said. "The world needs more Vasyas and Levs. They are heroes to me. And to many others. If I don't help them out, what good am I to anyone who stands up for freedom? It's time to be counted too."

Louisa looked deeply into my eyes, then put her cheek tight against mine. She was silent but I felt the interior battle going on between her heart and mind.

"Please don't worry, my love," I whispered softly. "I know what I'm doing."

"You won't take a single step without me. Promise?"

"All right."

"Promise?"

"Yes, I promise."

"You're the craziest man I've ever met."

"Let's make love on our little boat in the storm."

She purred irresistibly, closed her eyes and pressed her lips to mine. The lovemaking sounds we made drowned out the storm pounding outside.

Early the next morning while I was brewing a pot of fresh coffee, the telephone rang. It was Nicholas.

"Luke, the State Department doesn't want to criticize Russia or the Eastern bloc countries because they're trying to integrate them into what they call the European Home. My contact there even used an Eisenhower quote to justify their position. You know the one: 'If we are not making peace possible we are making war inevitable.'"

"Nicholas, that was not Eisenhower. It was JFK and what he said was this: 'Those who make peaceful revolution impossible will make violent revolution inevitable'. So those assholes at State don't get it? They won't lift a finger?"

"They don't want to get involved, Luke. And we don't have any recourse in the courts. They say all those Russian businesses Lev talked about are legit."

"Legit? You know they're not. What bullshit."

"Look, I can work on political exile visas for Vasya's wife and kid. I know people in the Embassy in Moscow, getting his wife and child out won't be a problem. Him, I don't know. I need more time."

"We don't have more time! We need to do something now!"

"I'm working on it, Luke. Why don't you do your part and write a recommendation for I.S., detailing all Vasya's political persecutions, the prisons where he's been, the papers his group has published. It'll help me to speed up Marina's case."

There was a long moment of silence, but Nicholas must have heard the sound of steam coming out of my ears.

"And Luke," added Nicholas, "please lie low."

"What do you mean?"

"Don't do anything stupid, like playing Sherlock Holmes. You think I don't know you? Let's talk soon, okay?"

"No, not okay," I began to say. "Nick, wait…"

The line went dead and he was gone without a good-bye. I hung up the receiver and stared at the telephone in silent rage. I peeked into the bedroom to see if Louisa was still asleep. She was. Then I dialed Masha's number and asked to speak to Lev.

"Here's what I found out," said Lev. "My friends tell me Tractor has an office on 10th Avenue. His company is called Petro-Gas Consulting Partners, though no one can get inside the building because it has security guards that stop everyone. But Tractor has breakfast alone at 7 am every morning at a place nearby on West 33rd Street. It's called Paris Café."

"Good work, that's excellent," I said in a low voice. "Lev, meet me at the corner of 33rd and 10th Avenue tomorrow morning at 6:30 sharp. Park your delivery van on the east side of the avenue, okay? I'll be waiting for you there. Please don't tell your cousin where you're going. And not a word about any of this to Nicholas or Louisa either. It's going to be just you and me, okay?"

"Luke, you sure you know what you're doing? Tractor is a very dangerous man."

"I just want to talk to him. Don't worry. He can't do anything in this country."

"Shouldn't we call the police, just in case?"

"No police," I said firmly. "They won't do anything because we don't have any evidence, at least not yet. We'll be fine."

Lev paused, taking a moment to reflect, then he said:

"Okay, Luke, I'll be there. I have never done anything like this before."

"Are you kidding? You fought these people in your own country. That's more dangerous than what we're doing."

"Luke, are you bringing a gun?"

"I don't own a gun, Lev. I'm a lawyer, I don't need one. We have laws in America. And a constitution. On the top of our Supreme Court building it says, 'Equal Justice for All.'"

"I thought everybody in America carried a gun."

"I hate guns, Lev."

"Tractor has one, that's for sure. Do svidanya.[21]"

"*Do vstrechi*[22]," I said with my terrible Russian accent.

---

[21] Goodbye.
[22] See you later.

WHAT HAPPENED NEXT was crazy and unexpected.

Louisa had work to do at her apartment and didn't stay with me that night, so I didn't have to tell her what I was up to, or involve her in anything risky.

At the crack of dawn on that cold, gray day, I took the 1 train down to 34th and walked over to 10th Avenue. It was too early for the usual buzz of commuters, pedestrians, cars and buses on 34th. Light, persistent rain was falling and an eerie silence blanketed the city. The cold wind that was blowing through the canyons of Manhattan chilled me to the bone.

While I waited for Lev next to a mountain of uncollected garbage bags, I scoped out the Paris Café and noticed a back door for deliveries that opened onto an alleyway behind the place. Lev arrived right on time, parking Masha's Kosher Deli van in a loading zone. I crossed to the driver's side of the van and Lev stepped out, looking pale and unshaven. His eyes were red, surrounded by swollen bags that told me he hadn't slept at all that night.

"You all right?" I asked.

Lev lit up a cigarette and didn't respond. After a couple of drags, he finally looked me in the eyes.

"Luke, you sure about this?"

"Yes, I am. Everything will be fine."

"Sorry, I just was thinking …"

Suddenly, I saw a taxi stop right behind the Kosher Deli van. Louisa stepped out of the taxi wearing a pair of tight-fitting black pants, a leather jacket and cowboy boots. My face must have signaled

211

my surprise because when I turned to Lev, he said: "I didn't tell her, I swear."

Louisa walked up to us with a devilish smile.

"We agreed," she said, "that you weren't going to do anything without me, remember?"

"I remember," I said.

"So?"

"This is nothing."

"Really? Well, Lev doesn't think it's nothing."

I turned to Lev, irritated.

"So you did call Louisa?"

Lev didn't answer me. He was pacing back and forth on the sidewalk in agitated thought.

"No, Luke," said Louisa with a wry smile. "Lev didn't tell me what was up. Masha did. Lev told his cousin where he was going with her truck. And I wanted to join the party."

"Thanks, my love."

"You're welcome."

Lev stopped pacing and said abruptly:

"Doesn't this situation look crazy to you, Luke? You and me trying to talk to Tractor?"

"We need to confront that jerk, otherwise they get away with whatever they want."

"Okay, okay," interrupted Louisa. "We're all here now. Let's get our ducks in a row. What's the plan?"

"It's changed a little. Louisa, you drive the van. Lev, give her the keys. You'll wait until 7:15, then go around the block and park near the back door to the diner. Wait for us there. Lev and I will go in, get a table and wait for Tractor to order breakfast. We'll approach him while he's eating, get information on Vasya's whereabouts, and ask him to help us get Vasya released. Then we walk out through the kitchen, hop in the van and we're gone. Plain and simple."

Lev lit up another cigarette and started puffing maniacally. He looked worried.

"I'll do the talking, but I need Lev with me in case this Tractor guy pretends that he doesn't understand English."

Louisa looked worried too. "And why on Earth do you think this guy is going to tell you where Vasya is?" she asked.

"We know where he is," I explained. "But we need this guy to use his KGB connections to help us get Vasily out of the asylum and out of the country.

"He's going to help you?"

"Sure," I said. "He has to. Otherwise we go to the press with what we know about his money laundering and the illegal business deals, okay? The last thing this guy wants is journalists asking hard questions. Right, Lev?"

Lev was silent.

"We have no other choice," I continued. "We can't go to the authorities. They're in bed with these people. And we're short on time."

"Lev, if you're not okay with this," said Louisa, "we can call it off. Now."

"I'm okay," said Lev, throwing his cigarette butt in the gutter. "Who said I'm not okay? I want to confront the bastard too. It's way overdue."

"Great," I said. "Let's get ready, it's almost time."

I kissed Louisa and she got into the van's driver seat, watching us through the windshield. Lev and I started walking towards the Paris Café. Still no sign of Tractor. The rain had stopped. More and more pedestrians appeared out of nowhere, carrying umbrellas and hurrying to their offices. The streets began filling up with cars and trucks.

As we turned the corner, with the entrance to the Paris Café in view, Lev suddenly stopped in his tracks. He was pale and his forehead was covered in sweat. I stopped, too, and saw him shivering.

"Lev, what's the matter?"

Without saying a word, Lev turned around and started walking away from me.

"Lev, wait, wait!"

Lev ignored my call, started jogging, and then broke into a full sprint.

"Lev! Lyova! Stop! Please!" I shouted.

I raced after him. Seeing us run down 10th Avenue, Louisa got out of the van and joined the chase. Lev zigzagged down the sidewalk through pedestrians, and barely stopped for red lights at the intersections. Louisa and I were both yelling at his back, pleading with him to stop.

Finally, three blocks down the street, Lev stopped abruptly, unable to breathe, and dropped down on the sidewalk, his hands covering his eyes.

When we reached him, he was gasping for air and sobbing.

"I can't do it," said Lev with a heartbreaking moan. "I just can't. I'm sorry, Luke, I'm so sorry."

"Don't worry." Louisa said breathlessly, kneeling down next him. "You don't have to do anything. You've been through enough."

She pulled out the hem of her blouse and wiped Lev's tears away. As she comforted him, she looked over at me, silently pleading with her eyes to call the whole thing off.

"Friends, I have hope now, for the first time in my life. Hope! I want to live! I want to be free from people like Tractor! I don't even know if Vasya is still alive!"

Lev's voice wobbled. "Oh, God, what am I saying?"

Louisa put her arm around Lev's shoulder and gave him a hug. I looked at my watch. It was 6:55. I couldn't stop now.

"All right," I told them. "You two wait for me in the van. This won't take long."

I turned around and walked back to the Paris Café to confront Tractor.

WHEN I GOT back to the entrance of the diner, there was a tall bald guy in a black suit standing outside the place wearing sunglasses. He was a conspicuous *homo-sovieticus* security man stationed there to look over everybody going in and coming out of the place. I put on my reading glasses and bought a newspaper at the corner kiosk. As I walked up the three steps to the Paris Café, the guy stared at me with his stony face, dismissing me immediately as a harmless intellectual.

I sat down at the breakfast counter and ordered a cup of coffee and a toasted bagel. Over the edge of my *New York Times,* I spotted Tractor sitting by himself in a red leather booth, reading the *New York Post* and eating an omelet with home fries. Despite his expensive business suite, I recognized the same guy who had me beaten up and dumped across the border into Serbia.

There was a steady procession of people coming in, ordering take-out and hurrying off to work. I took a sip of coffee and a bite of bagel, awaiting my chance to approach.

Suddenly I spotted Tractor getting up and walking back to the restrooms. Sensing this was my moment, I put down the newspaper, stood up and walked back to the restrooms as well. In the back hallway, the door to the men's toilet was shut tight. I saw the delivery entrance that opened up on the back alley at the end of the hallway and I quickly devised a new plan. I could feel the adrenaline start pumping through my veins. I waited for a few more moments, then I knocked on the men's room door.

"Not finished yet," I heard Tractor say from inside.

I knocked again.

"Not finished I said!"

I knocked one more time.

The door to the men's room opened wide open.

"Hey asshole," said Tractor, not recognizing me. "I said I'm not finished yet!"

"Yes, you are, Kravtsov," I said, pushing him back into the men's room and closing the door. He reached for a gun in his coat pocket and I delivered a hard punch to his liver that doubled him over. I grabbed his gun, a 9mm Beretta, put it on the sink and took out the pair of rainy day handcuffs I had brought along to the party. Another hard punch to his chest and he submitted to my cuffing his hands together behind his back, rendering him harmless.

I pushed him down to the floor with my foot on his neck, holding up the Beretta. At first he didn't recognize me.

"What do you want?" he babbled. "Who are you?"

He took a closer look at my face and his eyes widened in disbelief.

"You," said Tractor. "The lawyer."

"That's right, Kravtsov, it's me. Welcome to America," I said, waving his Beretta around. "Hey, bursting into toilets to assault people is a trick I learned from you."

I crouched down close to his face. "How does it feel on the receiving end?"

"This is bullshit!" mumbled Tractor.

"By the power of American common law, you're under citizen's arrest," I said. "Now get up and keep quiet."

"You can't do this, I'll…" Tractor started to say.

I punched him hard in the solar plexus, which shut him up.

"You'll do what? If you threaten me in my own country, I'll put a hole in your balls," I said, dangling the Beretta over his crouch.

That got his attention. I pulled him up off the floor, slipped the Beretta into my back pocket and opened the men's room door. Quickly I guided him out the delivery entrance to the alleyway where Louisa and Lev were waiting in the Kosher Deli van. Seeing Tractor coming out in handcuffs with me pushing him forward elicited panicked looks from both Lev and Louisa.

"Open the back of the van," I told Lev.

As soon as Lev opened the van's cargo door, I pushed Tractor inside and jumped in too, taking my place on a jump seat in the back.

"Drive!" I called out to Louisa.

The van accelerated like a sports car.

"Where to?" she asked.

"Take the Lincoln Tunnel. I'll explain once we're in New Jersey."

We rode along in silence, no one daring to utter a word. Tractor quickly regained his composure.

"What do you want from me?" he asked.

"I need your cooperation," I told him.

"I knew you were CIA."

"I'm not CIA. And I'm not FBI either. I'm FYA."

"What's FYA?"

"FYA is 'Fuck You Asshole' if you don't help us. We're going to make your American existence a living nightmare."

"Where are we going?" asked Louisa.

"Port Jersey."

"Why Port Jersey?"

"Cause it's nice and quiet over there. We can do anything we want with our Russian friend."

I looked directly into Kravtsov's hardened eyes.

"There'll be no witnesses."

I pointed Tractor's Beretta directly at his head.

"You have about 30 minutes to figure out how to locate and release our friend, Vasily Verbitsky. You know who I'm talking about, don't you? Your goons tortured him."

Tractor was staring at me with bewildered eyes, for he had always been the hunter, not the prey. The tables had been turned so abruptly that he was speechless.

"I repeat, Kravtsov," I said. "You are going to cooperate with us. Otherwise, I'm going to throw your sorry ass into the Atlantic Ocean right in front of the Statue of Liberty so she can take a dump on you while you drown."

"What are you doing, Luke?" said Lev. "Have you gone mad?"

"Maybe," I said. "But we're not going to let Vasily down."

Louisa said nothing as she focused on the road, looking at me worriedly in the rear-view mirror. I returned her glances with a look of confidence though I still wasn't sure what to do. Lev sat up front in the passenger seat and was silent as well. He turned around regularly to check out the incredible sight of Tractor sprawled on his stomach with his hands cuffed behind his back in the van. It smelled of pastrami and smoked fish back there. Lev's eyes shone with a mixture of fear and revenge. I reached over and patted him on the shoulder for comfort.

"Look at your Tractor now, Lev. We did it."

He grabbed my hand and shook it proudly.

Port Jersey is a large, flat, empty expanse of marshland next to the Hudson-Raritan Estuary dominated by the big cargo dock with its railroad cars, its stacks of containers being unloaded from freighters from all around the world and its rows of gigantic cranes looking like a monstrous tribe of mechanical praying mantises.

Past the port, Louisa pulled the van off the main road onto a gravel one and drove us into a marshy area near the bay. Seagulls were circling above the water. There was a signpost that said this desolate area was a bird sanctuary for terns. The van stopped, engine idling, near a concrete pier jutting out into the bay.

I looked at the now silent Tractor, one of strangest birds I'd ever encountered in captivity, and then exchanged quick glances with Louisa and Lev. The only sound now was the pitter-patter of rain that rolled over this isolated sliver of New Jersey coastline.

"Turn off the motor," I said to Louisa.

I waited for a few minutes until the rain subsided and opened the van's back door. Then I slipped the Beretta into my coat pocket and got out of the vehicle. I saw a thick black tire iron in the van and picked it up.

"Get out, Kravtsov," I said, tapping the iron against the bottom of his shoes. "Now we're going to get to the truth. One way or another."

Obeying my orders, Tractor slithered out the door with his hands cuffed behind his back. When he felt the ground with his feet, he stood up. Louisa and Lev came around to the back of the van and stood on either side of me. Tractor's small, venomous eyes looked the three of us over and, like a trapped animal, he quickly scanned the terrain for an escape route.

"No longer the infamous Tractor, right?" I said. "Here you can't bully innocent people, Comrade Kravtsov! And beat them up until they say what you want!"

"You've got the wrong person," he said. "My name is Ivanov, Alexander Sergeyevich Ivanov."

"Sure, and I'm Anna Pavlova," said Lev. "We know about the fake name you go under at your American company. And we know about your phony businesses."

I held up the tire iron in a menacing way, waving it at Tractor. Maybe for the first time in his entire life, Kravtsov felt a twitch of fear coursing his evil veins.

"Now are you going to tell us where you put Vasily Verbitsky? Or do I have to beat it out of you?"

There was a long moment of silence, and then abruptly, Tractor changed his tone.

"Okay, I'll tell you whatever you want. But then you've got to let me go."

"I don't think you're in any position to negotiate, Kravtsov," I said, poking him in the chest with the tire iron.

"Verbitsky was farmed," Tractor said, finally spitting it out like poison, though managing a little malevolent smile. "We tried to keep him alive."

"What do you mean you tried?" Lev yelled out.

"He's dead. Verbitsky cut his own wrists. There's nothing I can do about him now. By the way, he was a drug addict and an alcoholic. There are records to prove that it was a suicide."

Lev and I looked at each other in shock. Lev took a deep breath and closed his eyes in pain, bending over as if struck by lightning.

"We don't give a damn about your records, Kravtsov," I said. "They're full of manufactured lies anyway."

"We didn't know Verbitsky worked for you," said Tractor. "Otherwise, we could've made some kind of arrangement."

"He wasn't working for anyone except his own country. We're ordinary people, not agents. I'm just a lawyer!"

"Sure, ordinary people," said Tractor. "And I am a UNESCO ambassador?"

Tractor fixed Lev with a look of disgust but addressed me.

"What's he doing here anyway? Does this *zhid*[23] work for you, too? He's the one who signed all the papers on Verbitsky. We slapped him around a couple of times and he gave up everybody's names. He's lucky we let him go."

Lev quickly stood up tall and put his face only a couple of inches from Tractor's.

"Don't talk to me like that, you piece of shit!" Lev screamed at his nemesis. "Who did this to me?"

Lev held up his right hand with the mangled index finger.

"Your people tortured me and forced me to sign that confession! I would not do anything against Vasya! He was my best friend!"

Lev clenched his hand into a trembling fist and brought it close to Kravtsov's face.

"You think because you pulled my fingernail out, I'm afraid of you? I'm not! Hear me? I am not afraid of bloodsuckers like you! Not anymore! It's you who should be afraid of me now! You have blood on your hands! I hate you and all your KGB monsters!"

Though filled with rage, Lev slowly lowered his fist, his lips shaking, his face contorted with anger, fear and frustration. Thanks to all the years of non-violent resistance, he could not bring himself to strike Tractor.

Louisa took Lev's hand in hers to console him. Then she unexpectedly stepped forward and slapped Kravtsov hard across his face.

"That's from all of us," she said as Tractor's nose started bleeding a little. "You're a murderer!"

Louisa couldn't believe her own hostility toward this perfect stranger. It caused her to burst into tears.

"Lev, stay in the van with Louisa. I'm going to take a walk with our KGB friend."

---

[23] Kike.

"No, I'm coming with you," said Louisa.

"No, you're not! Get in the van and start the engine. Please!"

Louisa did as I asked, but she was not happy about leaving me alone with Tractor. I had the Beretta in my right hand and the tire iron in my left.

"Start walking, Kravtsov," I said. "Up on the pier."

Tractor obeyed. With me right behind him, he slowly walked up the ramp onto the pier, gazing around the marshland, hoping one of his security guards would show up and save him. At the same time, he was trying to guess my next move. Was I going to bludgeon him with the tire iron or shoot him with his own pistol?

I walked him right to the end of the pier. There I removed the handcuffs and turned him around to face me, getting all his attention by aiming the Beretta at his chest.

"Hey, Kravtsov, do you remember that speech you gave me on the border between Serbia and Romania?

Expressionless, Tractor was waiting for me to shoot him.

"No? Well, I do."

I pointed the tire iron westward, keeping my eyes on Tractor without blinking once.

"This is America. Our land. Our home. Your corrupt country is way over there."

I pointed the tire iron eastward.

"That's where you kill people who disagree with your regime. We don't eat each other over here, okay? We take care of each other. Americans live peacefully because we are free. Free, do you hear me? And we don't want people like you here. You do not belong. You can't get away with your illegal business bullshit in our country. And you can't benefit from laws that protect our freedom-loving people. Take your fucking business and go back to your own twisted Communist country. You drove Vasya to death, you and your scum secret police!"

Tractor's face was frozen. He was watching me like a mountain cat ready to pounce. I cocked the Beretta just in case he thought he could jump me.

"Make a move and I'll kill you like the stray dog you are, Kravtsov!" I said. "I'm not finished telling you what I think of you.

You've been killing the best and the brightest people in your country for decades. And now you turn up in our country? To do what? To make money? Go back where you came from and don't ever come back. Or we're going to expose your criminal activities."

"I can't go back home," Kravtsov said.

"And why is that?"

"Because the new Russian government under Yeltsin is after me. Are you working with them too?"

"Listen, Kravtsov, everywhere you look you only see secret agents. Here, people work for decency and truth. Maybe they fight corruption, or help the underprivileged or teach people about freedom. And you label them all foreign agents and try to get rid of them. There's no more USSR and yet you're exactly the same tyrants. Just dressed in business suits. You'll never change!"

"You're good," said Tractor, with the same raspy, menacing voice even though cornered like a rat. "I have to admit you're very good."

"I'm telling you I'm not an agent! We're ordinary citizens who decided to make a difference! And not put up with your totalitarian bullshit! Why is it so difficult for you to comprehend?"

"Okay, Mr. Robin Hood," said Tractor. "You know what I comprehend? That you're too weak to shoot me."

With that, Kravtsov let out a wicked laugh and dove backwards into the sea. Motionless, I watched him start swimming away from the pier, floating on his back, kicking with his feet. I took aim at him with the pistol, but I knew I'd never pull the trigger. I angrily threw Tractor's Beretta into the bay and watched it sink out of sight.

"I hope a shark eats you!" I called out.

"We will meet again!" Tractor shouted back.

I walked back to the van and got in.

"Somebody with a boat will pick him up," I explained.

"I can't believe you let him go," said Lev. "He should be punished."

"That's not my job, it's the government's. And the only way to make that happen is through the press. Nick is getting a reporter to publish a story in *The Washington Post*, using all your research. No one in their right mind would want to do business with Tractor and his pals anymore. They're going to have their hands full defending themselves in court against Federal indictments."

"That man is evil," said Louisa, starting the van's engine. "I'm glad it's over."

"He will be back," Lev mumbled. "I know it."

60

IT WAS STILL raining as I drove out of Manhattan and emerged on 495, impatient to get to Montauk. It seemed like it had never stopped raining for the last ten years. A thick fog from the Atlantic was rolling in again. Inside me, it had been 10 years of turbulence and fog as well. I wanted this trip to end one way or another, to get some emotional clarity. I was tired of throwing my life into the air like a juggler, not knowing if I could catch all the spinning plates before they came crashing down, unable to make a choice between my past and my present.

The last three and a half days behind the wheel seemed like a lifetime to me. The long-awaited reunion with my dream lady was only hours away. I almost wanted to postpone my arrival to savor that delicious moment. The horrible weather was not letting up, so whether I liked it or not, I had to slow down.

The daunting rhythm of raindrops on my windshield made it difficult to see the lanes on the Long Island Expressway, much less drive within them. Combined with the ghastly bolts of lightning shooting across the sky and the thunder splitting the black clouds above me, the storm distorted my focus. My eyes were glued to the road. Still, I needed time to collect my crazy, disparate thoughts.

So I got off at the next exit, Van Dam, and realized that I wasn't far from the Greenpoint section of Brooklyn and The Hole, the decadent lounge/bar where Louisa and I first met a decade ago. I decided to re-visit The Hole's decrepit neighborhood. That infamous watering hole was built inside an abandoned warehouse a couple blocks from the riverfront, its parking lot in the back was next to a dump strewn with rusty carcasses of broken-down cars. Once on Greenpoint, I took a right on McGuiness and drove a few blocks until I spotted Freeman Street. What a perfect address for The Hole! I made a left on Freeman and cruised down my own memory lane toward the East River.

The Hole and all the vacant lots had disappeared. The entire neighborhood had been transformed into something clean and modern, no longer funky and chaotic. It had been gentrified into neat apartment buildings and spiffy commercial spaces with newly-planted trees along symmetrical sidewalks. It was pretty but passionless.

Exactly where The Hole used to stand was a *magnus opus* of slick, tasteless architectural showmanship that sported aluminum panels, big glass windows and video cameras pointed at every imaginable angle. It was some kind of bank now, as it said "Credit Union" in big letters above the entrance.

I pulled over and let the car idle, listening to the rain, remembering fondly the dive where lots of tormented souls were searching for a little peace of mind, one night of horny pleasure, or an opportunity to simply forget everything including themselves. It was a place that gave yourself a break from yourself. And now, the lost souls had gone elsewhere and the neighborhood had become a shrine to greed. I wish I hadn't stopped and seen this travesty of modernization.

I pulled out and headed back to the expressway. It was time to move on in more ways than one. The rain and the fog made me steer cautiously along the highway. I was driving eastward through a contemporary landscape of shopping malls and car dealers, but I was thinking about what this land must have looked like hundreds of years ago when it was nothing by magnificent forests, pristine rivers and untouched valleys. This was the land of the Iroquois before the French and English fur traders showed up and decimated the native tribes with European diseases.

It took me until the ripe old age of 40 to find out that my maternal great-grandfather was an Iroquois Indian, a member of the Mohawk tribe. The Iroquois were called "Haudenosaunee" or the "People of the Longhouse" because that was how they lived, in long, narrow shelters with several families together.

I was never curious about my own heritage, but the Iroquois connection tickled my fancy. The Mohawks were warriors, developing arrows with flintheads to overpower their enemies. They were also known as the "Keepers of the Eastern Door" because for hundreds of years, Mohawks guarded the other Iroquois tribes against invasion from New England and lower New York areas. So it was perfectly possible that my ancestors hunted, fished and fought out here on Long Island in a past century.

I turned south at the Sagiktos Parkway and then caught Route 111 until I made a left on Route 27 near East Islip. The rain hadn't let up, nor had the fog lifted. There were fewer and fewer cars on the road. I was driving as if on automatic pilot, a pigeon flying home by some navigational magic.

The solitude made me think of my Mohawk great-grandfather. How would he have managed out here all alone in the darkness with rain coming down ceaselessly and fog clouding his view of the trail? The old Mohawk might have been thinking that that was the end of the world. He could have thought the Iroquois spirits were all going mad, that they had abandoned him, that the earth was condemned to hellish darkness and that the sun would be eradicated by the storm.

The old Mohawk wouldn't have been scared for his own life. He would have been worried about his loved ones back in the village, his wife and son who he had left behind to go on this hunt. Just like me, the old Mohawk must have been talking to himself a lot, asking for help and guidance.

I drove past Patchogue, Moriches, then Eastport. There wasn't another soul out here now. At Shinnecock Bay, the fog was so thick I had to slow the car down to a crawl.

A tremendous sense of guilt enveloped me like the fog. The same guilt must have crushed the old Mohawk's heart too. Why didn't he show more love to his wife and his child? Why did he leave them alone to strike out on his own into unchartered lands? The old Mohawk was probably worried he might die on this trail, battered and drowned by God's fury, abandoning his family for good.

Separated by a few centuries, I was on a lonely road having exactly the same thoughts as the old Mohawk.

Past Water Mill, Bridgehampton and then Amagansett, I pushed my car forward relentlessly. I wished the old Mohawk were riding shotgun in my car right now, dressed in one of those beautiful Iroquois outfits. We wouldn't have to talk. We would glance at one another, knowing how much we shared. We would understand the other without exchanging any sounds. It would be a peaceful, man-to-man thing. We would be fighting to survive from here on out. The rain and fog wouldn't throw us. Heaven and Hell couldn't scare us. All the Gods couldn't choke our manhood to death with guilt.

But the old Mohawk wasn't here. No one was out here but me. Where were all the cars on Route 27? Was everyone hunkering down at home just to escape the rapacious rain and fog? They didn't want to challenge the elements and risk triggering God's fury? They didn't want to push their luck?

Listen, you gods, I've always pushed my damn luck! And I know You like playing mind games with me. I don't care if You are laughing at me. One day I'll have the last laugh. I'll earn my own happiness without You!

I was lost in my thoughts as Napeague disappeared in the rear-view mirror. At the end of my tether and at the end of Long Island, that last stretch of road seemed to take an eternity to drive. Then suddenly, without knowing how I found my way through the rain, I spotted the fluorescent sign out front of Martha's Inn and pulled up in front. I turned off the car engine, grateful for the silence. The only sound I could hear were the waves breaking on a nearby beach.

My journey had come to an end.

61

I CLOSED MY eyes to savor the moment and leaned back against the head rest. I had driven up the entire East Coast of the United States to see her again. We were going to be together after ten long years without hardly a word from each other. Oh, Louisa, Louisa, the love of my life, now is our time!

I must have fallen asleep for a while because when I next opened my eyes, an ocean breeze had blown away the storm clouds and the first light of dawn was shimmering over the ocean.

Unlike New York City, nothing out here in Montauk had changed much. Martha's Inn was exactly as I remembered it, a 2-story New England-style brick structure with white shutters and a front porch stretching across the entire façade, trimmed with a white picket fence. The other buildings around here looked about the same as well, no worse for the wear despite constant pummeling by salty sea air. That welcoming smell of the nearby Atlantic permeated everything, just like before. The rising sun sent streaks of orange and gold across the azure sky, highlighting the long, narrow clouds high above the coast. It was all as I remembered it. I let out a muffled sigh, a mélange of awe with the beauty of it and relief that it still existed.

I got out of my car and walked slowly up the stairs to the front porch, looked around gratefully and listened to the silence. Not another soul was stirring yet. I pushed open the big wooden front door and walked inside, relishing the parquet floor, the rugs, the framed antique pictures, the hominess of the place. Ten years had passed in the blink of an eye. Martha herself appeared, coming out of the breakfast room holding a tray. Her make-up and hair were arranged impeccably. She was dressed like the 50s film star, Connie Francis, in "Jamboree," only with an apron.

"Welcome, to Martha's Inn," she said. "Do you have a reservation?"

Martha spoke with that same charming, slightly eastern European accent. I looked straight into her eyes. She blinked thoughtfully as she studied my face, trying to dredge up some vague memory that failed to come up. But she didn't recognize me. Why would she?

"Is the Jasmine Room available?" I said with a tired voice.

"Yes, the Jasmine Room is…"

Martha stopped dead in her tracks, almost dropping her tray and locked eyes with mine in sudden understanding. She was momentarily speechless. "Oh, my god, it's you," she blurted out, then gasped for a deep breath of air.

Her face changed from that of a professional hostess to one of genuine sorrow tinged with unexpected joy. She put her arms around me and gave me a warm hug.

"Luke, Luke," she managed to say, backing away and taking hold of my hands, suddenly finding her voice. "How are you? After all these years, my god, you're back! I'm so glad, especially after everything that happened, I really wanted to see you again."

"I'm good, Martha. How are you?" I said. But all I was thinking about was her turn of phrase, "especially after everything that happened." Obviously, my appearance had flustered the good woman. Martha collected herself skillfully:

"…Not bad, not bad at all," Martha was saying to me, though I wasn't really listening. Her voice was trying to break through the fog in my mind.

"My God, Luke, it's so good to see you again. I've thought of you many, many times over the years, and here you are!"

I didn't know how to respond, so I smiled and said nothing, blinking my eyes at Martha with acknowledgement.

"Silly me!" Martha continued. "I'm just chattering on like a parakeet. Let's sit down and talk later. You look tired. Go on up to the Jasmine Room. I'll bring you a cup of hot tea, all right?"

"Two teas, please, Martha," I corrected her.

"Two teas?" she said.

"Yes, I'm expecting someone."

"Expecting someone?" repeated Martha, looking a little lost.

"You know who."

"Oh, I see," she said warily, forcing herself to smile at me. "Well then, go on up. I'll see you in a bit."

Without any further delay, I climbed the wooden staircase, walked down the hallway and resolutely opened the unlocked door to the Jasmine Room. The key was in the lock and I left it there for Louisa.

The room was exactly as I remembered it. I breathed a sigh of relief. Kicking off my shoes, I walked over to the window and opened it. A sudden breeze of salty wind blew into the Jasmine Room bringing the music of the ocean with it. It was a soft yet violent melody, underscored by the backbeat of thunderous waves crashing against some rocky cliff not far away. The place was perfect, just like a decade ago.

Without taking off my clothes, I lay down on the king-size bed and pulled the quilt over me because the ocean breeze had an early morning chill. My heart was pounding away, exploding in my ears. She would show up soon, any time now. What was I going to say to her? Nothing! I would say nothing. Explanations would be useless. I would take off her clothes, go down on my knees and start kissing her toes, then work up from there, not skipping a square inch of her lovely body.

Later, I could tell her how much I had missed her. Maybe I could explain how I was only half-alive for all these years. Maybe I would crack some jokes and make her laugh that laugh again. I had missed more than anything else the sound of her laughter.

Then we'd kiss and make love slowly, so slowly that it would last almost forever. It would be one continuous lovemaking séance, locked in each other's arms, with me inside of her and her inside me, our mouths glued together, our tongues dancing voluptuously. There would be no more separation. Never again, not until we died together!

I closed my eyes and waited for her delicious arrival. Then I fell asleep blissfully.

WHEN I NEXT opened my eyes, the window was still open and the curtains were gently rippling. It was still dark outside, but a new dawn was coming. Though the sun had not yet risen, it was already tinting the sky outside a faint shade of pink and orange. It was hard to believe, but I'd slept through an entire day and night without budging.

I pulled off the quilt and saw that I was still fully dressed, lying alone in the big bed. I'd never even taken off my shoes. I turned on the light on the bed stand just to make sure my eyes were not playing tricks on me. No one else was there. No one had slipped into the bed with me. It was untouched except for the crater where I had sunk into comatose sleep.

"She didn't show up," I mumbled to myself over and over like a madman.

Questions were boiling up in my head. Why didn't she come? What happened? How could she have missed our rendezvous? Did she change her mind at the last moment? Was she all right?

There was a gentle knocking on the door.

"Come in," I said with great expectations.

It was Martha, wearing her apron. She opened the door, and carried in a breakfast tray loaded with coffee, breads and fruits.

"Good morning, Luke," she said warmly. "When I didn't see you yesterday, I was concerned. So I peeked in on you last night and saw you sleeping so peacefully I didn't want to disturb. You must have been very tired."

"She didn't come, did she?" I asked.

"Who didn't come?" said Martha hesitantly.

"You know who."

Martha put the breakfast tray down on the bedside table. Then she sat down on the edge of the bed. Her benevolent face turned into a mask of dismay and apprehension. She could barely hold back her tears. Wordlessly, she stared into my confused eyes, not knowing what to say next.

Her look told me that something was very wrong. I suspected it from the moment I'd arrived, but I had totally blocked it out until now. There was no denying it any more. I felt panic pumping through my veins.

"I thought you came to celebrate Louisa's birthday, Luke," Martha finally said.

"Louisa's birthday," I repeated. "What birthday?"

"Ten years ago, it was her birthday, don't you remember? I can never forget that night."

"Her birthday," I mumbled.

The words "her birthday" snapped my mind back from the fog of the last decade into the sharp sunlight of reality and truth. Almost simultaneously with my personal awakening, the sun emerged from the ocean outside, sending hot yellow rays through the windows of the Jasmine Room, bathing everything in warm sunlight.

Now I could see. Louisa wasn't coming. She was never coming. She never even intended to come. She didn't send me any new note about us meeting again at Martha's Inn, right here in the same room where our love was first celebrated. The note that she gave to me was ten years ago. Our ten-year reunion was a total fabrication of my own sick imagination. It was a story I had made up on my own, in some dark corner of my confused head. What did that say about my troubled mind? It said that it had been playing cruel games with me for a decade.

"Martha, I don't know what to say. I'm so mixed up. What's happening to me? How can this be?"

I was unable to stop the unexpected tears coming down my cheeks. I covered my face with my hands to hide my emotional breakdown.

"My dear Luke, I'm so sorry," Martha said, putting her tender, motherly hand on my shoulder.

"Luke, sometimes we get lost inside the labyrinth of our mind. Stay here with me for a couple of days, give yourself some time, let your mind accept reality."

"What reality?" I murmured to myself.

I closed my eyes and a whirlwind of dark questions whipped through my brain. I felt nauseous. Why was I there? What really happened? Why couldn't I remember anything about that night ten years ago? What was blocking my mind?

"God," I prayed silently, "please help me to get some clarity."

I was going crazy with the confusion, but I was terrified of clarity as well. I realized that I had to get out of here and breathe fresh air, clear my brain, find some answers. I told Martha how much I appreciated her concern, but I needed to take a walk and figure things out. As always, she was calm and understanding.

"Walk down to the lighthouse," she said on her way out.

"The lighthouse?"

Yes, that's where I needed to go. I'm not sure why, but I needed to see Montauk Point again, that premonitory on the coast past Martha's Inn where there was a stately lighthouse. I didn't know why, but that's where I needed to go. I was there once before but I couldn't remember when. I grabbed my jacket, rushed downstairs and leapt off the porch like a hungry tiger, fire in my belly, leaving my car parked in front of the Inn. The morning air was brisk and energizing.

I started walking along Route 27 out toward the end of the peninsula. A few cars slowed down, their drivers glancing curiously at me, probably some locals up this early to go fishing. They were wondering why anyone would be strolling along the sandy trail along Montauk Highway at this hour of the day in a blue suit and white shirt. But respectful of each man's personal journey, they left me in peace. I didn't even notice them. I wasn't sure myself why I was out here, but I knew deep down that I had to walk and walk and walk until I remembered.

I was listening to the seagulls above and trying hard with each step to go back ten years ago in my mind to what really happened that night.

At first, all I remembered was the fog. The weather that night made Long Island roads hard to see, even harder to drive. This morning's bright sunlight didn't leave any room for obfuscation. There wasn't a cloud in the blue sky to hide behind. Now I understood that inclement weather had helped me bury an essential chunk of my life for all these years.

I thought the end of this trip was Martha's Inn, but now I realized that my journey's end was the Montauk lighthouse built atop the cliffs of Turtle Hill in 1796 under President George Washington. Little things were starting to come back to me. I didn't think I had ever been out here, but I had. My strides were more confident because up ahead, above the trees on the side of the road, I could see the glass crown on the lighthouse looming above the coast. My footsteps were more assertive now with the lighthouse aiding my navigation. It had been a guide and warning signal to sailing ships, steamers, submarines and fishing boats for over two centuries.

I laughed out loud, a sort of insane cackle. Wasn't it crazy that a lighthouse had kept me in the dark all these years? I was walking but didn't seem to be getting any closer to where I was going, as if my mind wasn't connected to my body. I'd pushed my memories of that night so far down that now I couldn't dredge them up. Wasn't it ridiculous that I could remember obscure details of legal briefs in cases I argued years before, but couldn't remember that night a decade ago that had shaped me into the human being I was now.

Some internal GPS was guiding me right at this moment. I was energized with a force and purpose I'd rarely experienced in my lifetime. The smells of the ocean were drawing me toward its mysterious power. As I walked on, I allowed my feet to take command, almost sleepwalking, my eyes open, yielding to wherever God was guiding me, no matter what truths I discovered out here.

The morning sea breeze was brisk. Suddenly I was shivering, with goose bumps up and down my spine. I buttoned up my jacket and pulled the lapels up around my neck. Yet something inside of me wanted me to feel even more discomfort. I needed pain. I needed a powerful slap in the face and a strong kick in the ass to wake me up from this decade-old lethargy. I marched on. With each step, my mind started to peel away layers of mental bark that had hardened around my most intimate memories.

Images started coming back, just like the old-style developing trays where photographs magically appeared on sheets of chemically-treated white paper. I began by remembering words, sights, feelings. I was starting to bring it all into focus, parse it out and make sense of it.

Yes, that day was Louisa's birthday! That was it, of course, that's why it was such a special day for her. She had picked me up in her white Corvette outside the courthouse that Friday afternoon. She passed me a note right before I had pleaded several cases that day as a court-appointed attorney for defendants who couldn't afford legal counsel. I remembered now it was raining cats and dogs.

We had kissed and she had wiped the raindrops off my forehead. We were delighted to be together, regardless of the bumper-to-bumper traffic. Her note said that she wanted to go back to Martha's Inn at the end of Long Island, despite the weather, to celebrate her birthday at the place where our love was born. I lifted her hand momentarily from the shift stick and kissed it, wordlessly showing my acquiescence to her wish, deeply thankful for her love. I remembered thinking what a lucky man I was.

63

THE DRIVE THAT night was slow-going because of the rain and all the traffic leaving the city. The smaller roads on Long Island were equally congested, plus the fog was rolling in from the ocean. We didn't mind because every moment we spent together was magical. We listened to classic rock'n'roll on the car radio and chatted about all kinds of subjects, some serious, some silly. We started talking about romance, bouncing between medieval notions of chivalry and those magnificent paintings by Delacroix in the Louvre, somehow arriving at one of my favorite books from childhood, "The Last of the Mohicans" by James Fenimore Cooper. Louisa had read it and loved it too.

The conversation turned to clichés about men and women. We laughed about some of the more obvious irrational ideas that men have about women and women have about men.

"That one about women being more sentimental, honey, that happens to be true," she stated during one long traffic light. "All the rest are bunk."

"Is that so," I asked playfully.

"Babydoll, let me tell you something," said Louisa, suddenly dead serious. "Women need one thing and one thing only. And that's called love. We are alive when we love. And the more we are loved, the more love we need. That's why I want to go to Martha's Inn tonight, honey. I want to spend time with you in the Jasmine Room, our own private love shrine, and make sacrifices to the gods. I want to thank them for our love and ask them for their blessings for the future."

Louisa paused for a long moment. Her tone had lost all playfulness, her voice had become solemn. I looked at her. She gripped the steering wheel hard and then she said the most amazing thing:

"I'm pregnant with our child."

I remembered looking at her as if lightning had just struck me. My tongue froze solid in my mouth and I was speechless. My hair seemed to catch on fire and singed my brain. I wanted to scream out for joy or quote Shakespeare or jump off the top of a mountain. All I was capable of doing was to kiss her bare arm and stroke her neck. Nothing else was said for a long time during the drive. We were both astonished by her announcement. Waves of warm emotions washed over me, but I decided to wait until I could find the right words to express my feelings about her momentous news.

"I'm honored, my love," I managed to say. "I mean it with every atom in my body. When your inner and outer worlds meet, it's profound. It's marvelous. I've never been so happy."

I gently placed my hand on her warm belly and closed my eyes, listening to the Corvette purr along and imagining our future together. I was in a state of inner peace. No wonder I closed my eyes and slipped off for a while. When I woke up, we were just outside Montauk.

I turned to Louisa and her eyes glistened with alarm.

"What's the matter, darling?"

There were no street lamps out here and the fog had grown even thicker. A black SUV on the road behind us had its bright lights on and was driving strangely close to Louisa's Corvette. Louisa was squinting from the piercing high beam lights, so I twisted the rearview mirror upwards to give her some relief.

"What's going on?"

"That SUV has been behind me for a long time and just won't pass me, even when I slow down. It's like the guy is getting his kicks by tailgating me. He's a real nuisance!"

"Try again to let them overtake."

Louisa slowed down the Corvette. The black SUV followed suit and stayed directly behind us, refusing to go around us though there was no traffic coming the other way from Montauk Point.

I rolled down my window, stuck my hand out above the roof and rotated my finger, gesturing to the SUV driver to pass us. He ignored me and kept driving directly behind us.

We would be arriving at Martha's bed and breakfast in another 200 feet.

"Don't slow down," I told Louisa. "Whoever it is, I don't want them to know where we're going. Drive on past Martha's. Let's try to lose them."

Louisa shrugged and jammed down on the gas pedal, gunning the Corvette's engine at the same time as she shifted down to a lower gear. The sports car zoomed ahead, tires screeching. The acceleration pressed my head back into the head rest. The SUV sped up behind us. Louisa raced down Route 27, curving right and left for the next mile through the rain and fog. We came to Montauk Point and the lighthouse. All along, I glimpsed the black SUV pursuing us in the rearview mirror on the passenger side.

"It's still there," she said, her voice trembling.

"Pull over," I said. "I want to see who these people are."

"No, darling. I don't want to."

"Please pull over! This is ridiculous! Who do these people think they are?"

"Let's just drive, Luke. Back to Manhattan. Please. I can lose them. Maybe they're criminals, who knows what they want?"

"Stop the car. This is ridiculous. Who the hell do these people think they are?"

Louisa masterfully drove the Corvette around Montauk Point and pulled over on the driveway leading to the solitary lighthouse, spinning the sports car around so that we were facing the road. She kept both hands on the steering wheel and her foot on the gas pedal. Above us, the lighthouse's beam of flashing light circled through the foggy night.

In a few moments, the black SUV appeared and stopped directly in front of the Corvette, seeking confrontation and blocking us off from the main road. Its bright headlights blinded us. Its big engine idled powerfully.

I jumped out and started screaming at the SUV as I moved toward it.

"Hey asshole, what the hell do you think you're doing? Get the hell out of that fucking SUV, you idiot!"

As I reached the driver's door, I knocked on the tinted glass window.

"Hey, open up, asshole!"

No response.

Then someone struck a lighter on the far side of the front seat. As the lighter moved toward the cigarette hanging out of a man's mouth, I suddenly recognized that unforgettable face. It was Igor Kravtsov – Tractor – giving me a venomous look.

Before I knew it, the driver slammed his door into me, knocking me to the ground. Then he gunned the SUV's engine.

"Luke, are you okay?" I heard Louisa screaming.

I lifted myself up and screamed to her:

"Louisa, get out of here! NOW!"

Her Corvette didn't move. The SUV suddenly bolted forward and struck the Corvette head on, locking the sports car on its big steel bumper and pushing it backwards like a charging bull. It wasn't much of a match. I jumped up and ran after the two vehicles as they moved across the lighthouse grounds, bursting through a white picket fence.

The SUV kept pushing the Corvette toward the edge of the bluff that the lighthouse stood upon. It all happened in a few seconds, but I saw it in slow motion. The SUV thrust the sports car over the edge of the cliff and into the abyss below. I could hear Louisa screaming at the top of her lungs, then a loud crash, then an explosion reverberated, followed by flames shooting up into the foggy sky.

When I reached the big SUV, it was idling calmly at the edge of bluff, observing the chaos it had caused.

Tractor lowered the passenger window and waved at me, as if to say we were even now. I rushed at his side of SUV, but the tinted window was already closed tight when I got there. I punched at the window and grabbed the door handle, but the goon who was driving the SUV threw the vehicle into reverse, spinning around and throwing me to the ground. The murderous SUV sped away into the night.

I stumbled to the edge of the bluff. The Corvette lay upside down like an old rag tossed on the beach below. White smoke was coming out of its engine. I screamed in agony, roaring like a thousand men, but my calls for help were drowned out by the waves breaking on the coastline. No one could hear me.

Scrambling down the big rocks as best I could, I got down to the bottom of the bluff after stumbling a couple of times on slippery rocks. Blood was coming down the side of my head and both my legs were bruised, but the adrenaline pumping through my body made me forget my own pain.

I got to the driver's side of the car, reached in through the broken window and put my hand on Louisa's cheek. She was unconscious but still breathing.

"Louisa, Louisa, my darling!" I moaned. "Stay with me! Stay with me!"

The door on the driver's side was twisted and jammed shut. By using both hands and leveraging my feet, I managed to get the passenger door open and reach inside the shattered Corvette with both arms.

I dragged Louisa out on the beach. She was like a broken doll. I cradled her in my arms and felt for her pulse. Thank God, she was still alive.

"Please help! Somebody, please help us!" I screamed up at the solitary lighthouse as loud as I could. "Help! Somebody! Help!" I kept yelling until there was no more air in my lungs.

The rain had weakened to a drizzle and the fog cleared. I made myself listen to any sounds of help arriving, but there was an eerie silence blanketing the coast. Even the waves became motionless. We were on our own.

I cupped Louisa's face in my hands, trying to shield her from the raindrops. When my hands touched her face, her eyes fluttered. Her faint breathing was painful, probably due to a punctured lung. Her clothes were soaked with blood. But the worst part was that her neck had been broken. Her shattered body was lying in my arms, paralyzed from the neck down and unresponsive. Yet by some miracle, she was able to move her lips ever so lightly and manage a faint smile.

"Louisa, my love, please, stay with me," I murmured into her ear. "I beg of you please! Don't leave me, darling!

Her bloody lips trembled. As gently as I could, I leaned over and kissed her. While I pressed my lips to hers, she exhaled one last breath into my mouth, then shuddered and was gone.

64

FOR ALL THESE years, I had blotted out the painful memory of that drive to Montauk in Louisa's Corvette and her violent death. My solitary walk today out to the tip of Long Island with the sun shining and the sea breeze tossing my hair around had jumpstarted the process of remembering.

All day long I sat in silent mediation at the top of the bluff under the lighthouse putting it all back together. The rest of that fateful night had surfaced like a riptide rising from the bottom of the ocean, carrying me away with long-suppressed images. It was the first time since that night ten years ago that I'd been back here emotionally as well as geographically. By quietly focusing, I had finally been able to dredge up the painful scene of Louisa dying in my arms. The setting today was diametrically opposite from that rainy, foggy night. It was beautiful out here this afternoon, with families walking down the sun-dappled beach, children tagging along, and dogs running along the surf below the big red and white lighthouse tower.

Lost in my past, I had hardly noticed the hours going by as the sun moved across the sky and descended in the west. The day had passed as effortlessly as one of those big fluffy clouds that drift by in the sky above the Atlantic. Evening was not far away because there was suddenly a chill in the air. I had been sitting here hour after hour quietly staring down at the exact spot on the beach where I was holding her that night, going over and over what really happened. It had all finally come back to me.

I hugged her lifeless body in my arms that night, trying to hold off the coldness that would surely come now that her heart had stopped beating. My dream woman and our child were gone forever. I didn't want to ever let go of her.

"NO, NO, PLEASE, NO!" I kept moaning in a primeval voice that had never come out of my mouth before, a mélange of sobbing and howling. I would have stayed there with her like that all night if I hadn't heard voices at the top of the bluff and seen flashlights up there. Some men dressed in overalls were calling out to me. A woman was giving orders. It was Martha, from the Inn, also dressed in overalls. She was a captain in the town's volunteer fire department. Somebody had heard the ruckus at the lighthouse and alerted the authorities. Police cars soon showed up along with an ambulance.

The rest of that night was difficult to remember in any certain chronology. I could still see medics from a nearby hospital prying Louisa's body out of my arms and carrying her up the bluff on a stretcher. Somebody put a blanket over my shoulders and asked me to come along. Later somebody else placed a mug of hot tea in my trembling hands. A man in a uniform, maybe a sheriff or constable, asked me how the accident happened. I remember mumbling to him:

"What accident? This was murder, plain and simple."

Somebody guided me to an ambulance that drove me to the local hospital. A medic laid me down on a stretcher and gave me an injection. I remember a siren screaming in the foggy night and flashing lights, then nothing. I had dropped into some sort of drug-induced unconsciousness.

Night was now falling quickly on Montauk Point and everyone had disappeared from the beach below. It now belonged to me and my souvenirs. So I climbed down the rocks, just like I did that night ten years ago, and sat down again on the beach where I had sat that night, where I had held her for the last time.

Alone now, I looked out at the dark sea and its perpetual waves breaking on the shore. There was hardly a whisper of wind. The night sky was filled with millions of stars. Watching all this unfold was mesmerizing. My skin was tingling and I could feel my heart beating hard in my chest.

It was one of the most powerful moments of my entire life, as if God was looking over me in all His dark beauty. And I was touching

His mighty feet on this tiny patch of sand. I felt like I was on the verge of facing my ultimate truth, when God revealed Himself and showed me my real purpose in life.

Everything became so crystal clear. I reached into my pocket and took out the Panasonic voice recorder that Louisa had given me. Now I understood that I'd been speaking to her through the recorder for all these years. That was over now. I no longer felt the need to push the red record button. There was nothing else left inside me to say.

The poor device looked bedraggled, as if it was on its last leg, ready to give up the ghost the next time anyone tried using it. I built a little totem to my Panasonic by stacking up some smooth stones on the beach. The voice recorder had served me well, living with me for all these years and listening to my soul-searching *ad nausea*. But that was all over now.

"I love you, my dear recorder, but I will leave you here," I said to the worn-out device as I placed it carefully on top of my memorial totem. "We must part ways here."

I stood up and faced the ocean. My last soliloquy was addressed to the heavens above:

"God, this is your humble servant, Luke Forsythe. The one who you've been avoiding all these years. You took my love away from me. And now You expect me to continue my life as if nothing happened? How can that be? I don't want to live anymore in this crazy world where You created so much misery and suffering. The buck stops with me here and now."

I took off my jacket and lay it next to the totem. I made sure my wallet and cell phone were in the jacket so they would be able to identify my body later.

"No answer, as usual." I continued. "Being silent is not going to cut it this time. I've had it with You. I do all the talking, all the living and all the suffering. All You do is observe? My decision has been made. I'm going to meet Louisa again. She's here. I can feel her. I want to be together with her forever."

Intently, I listened for something, a sign, a hint, anything. But there was only the continuous sound of waves breaking upon the shore. That was all I needed. I walked straight into the ocean and kept walking until the water was waist high. A wave came up out of nowhere and slapped me across my face, as if to tell me to turn around and go back.

I laughed. I wasn't afraid of anything anymore. The ocean was cold but that was fine by me. I was completely at one with the world. I swam further away from the shore. I paused, treading water, and looked up at the beautiful star-filled night. Then I took one last deep breath. Pulling my hands up, I let myself sink down into the dark water. The deeper I went, the colder the water. My lungs were fighting for air. The end was near. I could feel it. Or was it the beginning of something grander? All I had to do was open my mouth and take one last gulp of the ocean.

Except at that very moment, I heard Louisa's voice, clear as a bell:

"No, my love, I'm alive in you. Stay, stay, stay..."

Then God's little finger caused the undertow to grab me like a feather and push me up to the surface. Gratefully I gasped for air. I floated there, thankful to breathe again, unsure of what to do next. Wave after wave were pushing me back toward the shore. Louisa's message was clear. I obeyed her, paddled back and walked up on the beach.

As soon as I got out of the ocean, I started shivering. I found the totem, took off my wet shirt and put my jacket back on for some warmth, coughing up salt water. Without warning, I started crying, wailing like a wounded animal. The truth of this day had been too much truth for me to bear. I was crying so hard that I could hardly breathe.

Then suddenly my cell phone rang.

Really? Talk about terrible timing. This couldn't be happening. I ignored the phone at first, but the ringing was insistent, then it stopped. But whoever it was was calling me back again. I grabbed the cell phone from my coat pocket with trembling hands and looked at the display. It read "Home." I picked it up.

"Hello. Daddy?"

"Julian?"

I was still coughing up salt water.

"Daddy? Where are you? Why are you coughing?"

"I'm here," I said, gathering myself. "I'm here, son. I'm so happy to hear from you, son."

"Daddy, I'm just calling to remind you that my choir concert is Friday. You're going to come home in time, aren't you?"

"Yes, of course, son. I wouldn't miss it for anything in the world."

"Daddy, are you all right? Are you at the beach? I can hear waves in the background."

"Yes, Daddy is at the beach, son. I will be there for your concert, I promise."

"You're the best daddy in the world. I love you!"

"I love you too, Julian. I love you so much. See you soon. Now pass me your mom."

I couldn't stop the salty tears that kept coming. I didn't want to hold them back anymore. It was uncontrollable and liberating. There was silence on the line and some shuffling sounds, then I heard Margaret's voice.

"Is that you, my dear?" I said, my voice full of ancient sorrow and wisdom.

"Yes, honey, it's me. We miss you down here. I'm so glad you picked up the phone. We've been trying all day to reach you."

I could hardly put words together. I wiped my tears away.

"Darling, speak to me, please. Why are you crying?"

"My dear, dear Margaret," I was finally able to say, getting a grip. "I don't deserve you. I really don't."

"Where are you, darling? At the accident site?"

"Yes."

"I knew that's where you were going. You had to go back there, didn't you?"

"Yes," I managed to say. "But now it's done and I'm coming home. It's over."

We were both crying together now.

"Come home, my love. Please come home."

"I love you, my darling Margaret."

"We're waiting for you, Luke."

65

THE SCHOOL CONCERT was just starting when we arrived. Inside the auditorium we found two seats in the back among all the parents and relatives of the little boys standing so tall and perfect on the stage in their blue choir robes. The celestial voices of Julian and all the other boys singing *Miserere* together was enthralling. Julian saw us come in and a beautiful smile took over his angelic face. I squeezed Margaret's hand.

I had only just flown in a few hours before and I hadn't had time yet to talk to Margaret about my trip to Montauk. I left my car with Martha to use as she saw fit. It was near the end of its tether after my East Coast drive. Martha took me to the MacArthur Airport on Long Island and hugged me goodbye.

There was so much that I needed to tell my wife.

"Your palm is sweating," Margaret whispered. "You okay?"

"Yes, just happy to be here with you."

I stared at Margaret's hand resting on mine. Then I closed my eyes. I heard the beautiful choir music and felt the gentle weight of her hand.

"This is real," I thought to myself. "My wife's hand is holding mine. She has shown herself to be such a courageous woman. She knew I had to make that journey to remember my past and she let me go deal with it on my own terms. Her quiet love and support were there every mile of the way, even when I was scared, unsure and confused. I am so sorry to have caused her pain and anxiety."

I squeezed Margaret's hand and we exchanged a knowing glance. Everything was the way it was before I had left for Montauk. And that's the way I wanted it. I was home in the most complete sense of that word. I was a better man for having made that journey. But nagging thoughts still kept coming up. Was it all only a dream?

With my other hand, I reached into my pocket, felt the bruised Panasonic voice recorder in there and squeezed it appreciatively. Maybe the answer was in there.

T H E   E N D

Thank You ...

TO MY LITERARY agent, editor and friend, Jerry Rudes. There would be no *Lovers in the Fog* without Jerry's watchful eye over every single word of this book.

To the late Hercules Bellville of Recorded Picture Company, who took me under his wing and encouraged me to write the original version of *Lovers in the Fog*.

To my late teachers, Leslie Stevens (creator of "Outer Limits") and Conrad Hall (masterful cinematographer), for their belief in me as a storyteller.

To my father, Soviet dissident Vache Sarkissian, who has been the guiding light of my life and whose been my inspiration for Vasya Verbitsky's character in these pages.

To my daily muse and love of my life, my wife, Nathela, for her unequivocal support in writing this story and to my children Elisa, Lucas and Arpy, for their unconditional love.

To Jonathan Davenport and Andrew Cremeans for their inspirational artwork.

To my wonderful audio team for their generous support in creating the audio book of *Lovers in the Fog*:

* Steve "The Deacon" Hunter (renowned for his guitar work for Lou Reed, Genesis, Alice Cooper and Joe Cocker) for creating the original score for the audio book.

* Christopher Harvengt and Charles Maynes who sound-designed, edited and mixed the voluminous materials.

* David Cooley for his wonderful voice in the audio book.

For more information on how to buy both the book and the audio-book, please visit www.loversinthefog.com

About the Author

BORN IN 1962 in Yerevan, Armenia (the USSR at that time), Hamlet Sarkissian is the son of prominent Soviet dissident Vache Sarkissian who spent 18 years in Soviet gulag camps and KGB prisons. Vache Sarkissian ended up writing 3 novels, a 1,500-page triptych under the unifying title of "Akeldama" ("Blood Ranch"). As a teenager, Hamlet became the typist and underground distributor of his father's "samizdat" novels, joining his father's fight against the communist regime. Vache Sarkissian's clandestine works became underground hits, and as word spread about their frankness, demand grew for more copies. Russian authorities organized a witch hunt and confiscated most of the copies in circulation. In 1985, Hamlet was accepted at the prestigious Leningrad Institute of Theatre, Music and Cinematography. His studies were cut short by his father's suicide in 1987. The suicide of his father became a turning point in Hamlet's life. Life became unbearable in the Soviet system after witnessing his father's struggles firsthand and the falsehoods of the KGB-run propaganda machine. In 1989, Hamlet seized on an opportunity to immigrate to the U.S., sponsored by the International Institute of Human Rights. Since then, he has lived in Los Angeles with his wife, French writer, Donatella Gomelsky-Guichard, with whom he has three children. Hamlet is author of many short stories, plays and screenplays. He is also a filmmaker, having written and directed the award-winning feature drama "Camera Obscura" (2000). "Lovers In The Fog" is Hamlet's first novel.